LOOKING BACK
AN AUTOBIOGRAPHICAL JOURNEY
THROUGH SOUTH EDINBURGH AND BEYOND

LOOKING BACK
AN AUTOBIOGRAPHICAL JOURNEY THROUGH SOUTH EDINBURGH AND BEYOND

Charles J. Smith

Foreword by
Professor William A. Turmeau, C.B.E., F.R.S.E.
Former Principal of Napier University

MALCOLM CANT PUBLICATIONS

In memory of my wife
Catherine
and happy family days

First published in 2000 by
Malcolm Cant Publications
13 Greenbank Row Edinburgh EH10 5SY

Text copyright © Charles J. Smith, 2000

ISBN 0 9526099 4 0

Typeset by Hewer Text Ltd, Edinburgh
Printed and bound by Redwood Books, Trowbridge, Wiltshire

Contents

Foreword

Looking Back is the celebration of a life spent almost entirely in Morningside. It is a long life too, for its author is now in his 80th year.

Reading his autobiography will evoke in every Morningsider, and especially in the elderly ones, memories of a time that is past: little cool boxes hung outside the windows in the days before fridges were commonplace, the boys playing football in the street and the girls playing peevers, coal being carried up flights of tenement stairs and sheep arriving at the goods yard in Maxwell Street. In some of his local readers he will no doubt revive sad memories of those who did not return from World War Two.

Yet how the past is linked to the present. Stand at the gates of South Morningside School on the first day of the school year and I am sure you will still see the little five-year-olds clinging to their mothers' hands as did the young Charles Smith. Newspaper boys still tend to become more attentive on the run-up to Christmas! And I expect the Morningside pocket money still fails to satisfy all the needs of Morningside children.

Charles Smith has proved himself a close observer of his neighbourhood. Shops, schools, sports, and major festivals like Christmas and Hallowe'en jostle for space in his pages. The Church, The Boys' Brigade, and other youth activities feature prominently. Not only did Charles Smith observe, but he also contributed considerably to the community with his work for the Young Christian Workers' Movement and the Kilbrandon Council, and as a Community Development Officer.

The most fascinating chapter for me is the one recounting his years in the Medical School Bacteriology Department at the University of Edinburgh. How far medicine has progressed since his early days there. Or has it? As he points out, tuberculosis is again on the increase.

Finally, how fortunate it is for Edinburgh and Morningside in particular that Charles Smith became interested in local history. *Looking Back* describes his work as a writer, lecturer and researcher. Without the efforts of people like him, and his brother Bill, whom I knew as a senior lecturer in Physics at Napier University, it is all too easy for people and places and anecdotes to fade away beyond recall. These memories and reminiscences provide a lasting and comprehensive history which the close-knit community of Morningside needs and deserves.

I feel privileged to have been invited to provide this foreword, and to know Charles Smith whom I truly think of as 'Mr Morningside'.

Bill Turmeau,
Edinburgh, March 2000

Introduction and Acknowledgments

WHEN I eventually, and slightly reluctantly, agreed to Malcolm Cant's persuasive but flattering suggestion that I might consider writing an informal autobiography, I did so simply in the hope that what I had to say about my involvement in various events and enterprises might be of interest to others. The very last thing I wanted was for this venture to look like an ego trip. After a series of preliminary meetings with my publisher, we agreed the general framework for the book and I began to draw the threads together at the beginning of 1999.

I have to express sincere appreciation to many people for their assistance and advice in bringing this book to fruition. As the story is very much concerned with my family I must record my indebtedness to my daughters Barbara and Pauline and my son Charles for reminding me of events in the early days at home and in our travels abroad. I was constantly, but diplomatically, advised on what to put in and what to leave out.

A great deal of my life has overlapped with that of my brother Bill and his family. I am most grateful to him for keeping me right on some of the details of the early days which he remembered more accurately than I did. He contributed a lot of information on our family tree which he had already begun to record. Many early photographs, particularly of the family, have come from his carefully preserved collection. He also contributed to our boyhood

memories in Maxwell Street and our years in The Boys'
Brigade. I also welcome this opportunity to express again
my appreciation of Bill's valuable professional help with
regard to photographs and slide projection during my
many lectures to various groups and societies. I am also
happy to place on record his constant assistance in the
preparation of my earlier books, the trials and tribulations
of which have all produced interesting material for this
present book.

As with my previous research, I have again been greatly
indebted for the ready assistance of the staff of Edinburgh's
Public Libraries, both at the Edinburgh Room at the Central
Library and at Morningside Library. I am grateful to Mrs
Margaret McGregor who was a member of our earliest
infants' class at South Morningside School for lending a
photograph of these early days. It was a pleasure to trace
the family of the late Rev. Bill Whalley: his daughter, Mrs
Eleanor Gibson of Prestwick, and his son, Michael, (an
athlete like his father) now resident in Bermuda, both kindly
lent me photographs of their father.

I acknowledge the valuable assistance of the Medical
Illustrations Department of Edinburgh University, especially Ms Sandra Conner and Ms Nicola Greenhorn, and
also Mrs Sally Campbell, former youth worker at the Hyve.
The task of tracing information on the 'Dutch Lunches' at
Shandwick Place was made much easier by the ready
assistance provided by Ms Karine Macaulay, Personal
Assistant and Administrator to the Royal Norwegian Con-
sul General in Edinburgh, and also Norman Weibye, son of
the Norwegian restauranteur, Helge Weibye, who hosted
these events. In this day of computerisation I was fortunate
to have my manuscript converted to disk by Ingrid and
Douglas Gould.

Emeritus Professor J. G. Collee, CBE, my former Head of

Department in the Medical School, reviewed the chapter on my career in the University of Edinburgh.

I am also grateful to Professor William A. Turmeau, CBE FRSE, former Principal of Napier University for kindly writing the Foreword to this book. Morningside has cause to be grateful to Professor Turmeau for saving Craighouse, formerly the very historic part of the Royal Edinburgh Hospital, from an otherwise uncertain future by establishing there the Craighouse Campus of Napier University. He was also instrumental in ensuring the future of the former building of Morningside Parish Church by locating there Napier University's Morningside Campus.

Finally, my publisher, Malcolm Cant, has been of great encouragement. His valuable guidance and editorial skill, tempered with much appreciated patience, improved and brought my story to life.

Charles J. Smith Hon. B.Sc. (Edin.), FIMLT
March 2000

ONE

The Early Years

IF MANY Cockneys proudly claim to have been born within the sound of the Bow Bells, I might likewise claim a similar affinity with the great bell which hangs in Pilkington's Barclay Church on Edinburgh's Burgh Muir.

I made my entry into south Edinburgh on Wednesday 16 June 1920 in an area basement flat at No. 9 Glengyle Terrace, on the periphery of Bruntsfield Links, and under the towering 250-foot-high steeple of Barclay Church. I was baptised in the McCrie Roxburgh Church in Davie Street, which is now used by the Apostolic Church. The McCrie Roxburgh, where both my mother and father sang in the choir, had its origins in the Free Church of Scotland.

My mother, Johan Ranken, had been, before my birth, a counter charge hand and window-dresser with John D. Blair and Son, drapers and ladies' outfitter, at Nos. 1–3 Nicolson Street. Her family lived at East Adam Street, in a tenement building which has since been demolished. My father, Charles, who had lived in St Leonard's Street, was a commercial clerk with Parkinson and W. & B. Cowan, gas meter manufacturers, in Buccleuch Street. When they became part of the notable Parkinson–Cowan firm, the organisation moved to Manchester. My father always regretted how the workers in Cowan's in Buccleuch Street had been anxious about rumours of a close-down and had not been properly informed until after the deal had been concluded. He was offered the opportunity to transfer to Parkinson–Cowan in Manchester but chose to remain in Edinburgh and, therefore, became unemployed. Parkinson–Cowan's factory was duly demolished and the New Victoria Cinema (now the Odeon) was built on the site in 1930 with its frontage in Clerk Street. Today, modern flats also occupy part of the area.

My maternal grandfather, William Ranken, was employed at the Waverley Station as a porter with the North British Railway. He married my grandmother, Sarah Jane Elliot, from the Jesmond Dene area of Newcastle-upon-Tyne, but, despite research by the family, we have never discovered how, or where, they met. When they were married, they lived in Edinburgh, first at Forrest Hill, off Forrest Road and then at East Adam Street.

On the other side of the family, my paternal grandfather, also Charles, was employed to collect money from householders who had opted to pay by instalments, for goods supplied by various firms in Edinburgh. In his spare time he wrote lengthy essays on quite fundamental subjects, such as religious issues and what he saw as the 'natural rights of man'. His treatise, *Origin and End of Worlds*, in his own copperplate writing, is still held by my brother. In 1921 he went to Dublin to fight against the Black and Tans, a specially recruited armed police force sent by the British Government to deal with the Irish Troubles. He was an accomplished organist and composer, and also produced some fine examples of fretwork, particularly a Noah's Ark and a railway engine, the former now being in the Museum of Childhood in the High Street.

After he married my grandmother, Isabella McWatters, a seamstress from Dundee, they lived, to begin with, in the St Leonard's district of Edinburgh. I suppose that at the end of the nineteenth century many families were fairly static as regards work, residence and travel. My grandparents were not, however, quite so lucky. Around 1898 a business venture, for which my grandfather had acted as guarantor, failed, with far-reaching consequences for him, his wife and their three sons. Without warning, my grandfather came home one day and, without discussion or planning of any kind, announced to my grandmother that the family would be leaving for London immediately. Among the very few possessions which they took with them was my grandmother's small sewing machine. They left from Leith on one of the regular sailings which, even in good weather, took a few days. As they had no friends in London my grandfather had no option but to look for accommodation which turned out to be two modest rooms to rent in the Taplow Street area of Islington. My grandfather found work, my grandmother used her treasured sewing machine to earn a little cash doing repairs, and my father and his two brothers attended the local school. This must have been a very traumatic experience for the boys as I remember in later life that my father often recounted his days at Taplow Street with graphic details of how the teacher had told the class that people in Scotland still lived in caves! Around 1903 the family returned to Edinburgh's South Side where my father attended Preston Street School. Many years later, in the 1970s, my brother Bill took my father to revisit Taplow Street where he had once lived, only to discover that much of the area had been demolished for redevelopment. I am reliably informed, however, that the district features in the words of the famous rhyme

> Up and down the City Road
> In and out the 'Eagle'
> That's the way the money goes
> Pop goes the weasel.

The Eagle was a public house near Taplow Street and the weasel was the name for a lady's fur which had to be 'popped' into the pawn shop after too many visits there!

Back in Edinburgh, when I was about two years old, I am
sure that my father and mother had a much easier time
when we moved from the family home in Glengyle Terrace,
across Bruntsfield Links, to a top flat at No. 6 Livingstone
Place, a street which takes its name from the famous
missionary-explorer. At this stage, my father was still
employed by Parkinson–Cowan. I recall little of life at
Livingstone Place, save that my father took me down
regularly to play football on the Meadows. Any hopes that
he might have had of my achieving professional status in the
game, and perhaps earning big money, were not to be
realised! Playing for Edinburgh Boys' Brigade against Leith,
Stirling and Glasgow was the sum of my achievement in the
world of football.

When I was about three years old, we moved from
Livingstone Place for a few months to the pleasant little
village of Cramond, as my mother was in poor health and it
was hoped that she would benefit from the rest and the sea
air. We lived in a small house just a little way down the
steep steps between Cramond Glebe Road and the Shore,
from where my father still travelled daily to his work at
Cowan's in Buccleuch Street. I later learned that the land-
lord of this house (and other property in Cramond) was
Jimmy Cant whose family still reside in Edinburgh. I have
never lost a special love for Cramond and its unspoiled
charm.

Another reason for the family move to Cramond was that
in the previous year, just before Christmas, I had contracted
diphtheria which was a very common childhood illness in
those days before immunisation. I had been transferred by
ambulance (more commonly known then as 'the black van')
to Ward 14 of the City Fever Hospital at Greenbank. In
later years, I described to my parents my recollections of
being in the hospital, and of seeing them and friends looking

into the closed ward through the large glass panel in the doors.

At Livingstone Place, I certainly do not recall being aware of the other side of the Meadows with the great complex of the Royal Infirmary's peninsular, castellated wards. Middle Meadow Walk and the Medical School also seemed very far away but were to feature later in life. There was, of course, no university high-rise 'city' in the secluded, leafy George Square of old. Nor, at that time, was I aware of the significance of the collection of ruined stones in St Catherine's Place on the other side of Sciennes Road. Eventually, I discovered that they were the remains of the sixteenth-century Convent of St Catherine of Siena which gives its name to the district of Sciennes. Many years later I was to write an account of this religious house, and to conduct groups around the site, and the surrounding district, when I organised walkabouts for the students of Edinburgh University Extra-Mural Department.

In 1924 my parents and I and my younger brother Bill, who had been born earlier that year, moved further south across the old Burgh Muir to a second-floor flat at No. 3 Maxwell Street, where my life-long associations with the pleasant suburb of Morningside began.

Until the beginning of my school days, my experience of Morningside was confined to gazing down from our sitting room window to the busy street. Busy, in those days, but hardly at all with cars, as now. Most of the traffic at the west end of Maxwell Street was associated with the bustling coal yard, as we called it, or railway goods yard, a large siding off the suburban line, near Morningside Road Station. Large covered railway wagons arrived here to take potatoes, turnips, hay and other produce from the many farms around Morningside to the markets at Market Street beside the Waverley Station. Later, open wagons also arrived, bringing coal to be bagged by the various coal merchants who had huts in the goods yard. The bags were checked on a large weighing machine and then taken along Maxwell Street in horse-drawn carts for delivery to the villas and high tenements in the surrounding streets. Housewives, on hearing the welcome cries of 'Coal! Coal!' would lean out of their tenement windows and signal down to the vendors the number of bags required. In the present day of the Health and Safety Executive and other improved working conditions, it seems incredible that men climbed steep tenement stairs, often up to the fourth floor, with a hundredweight bag of coal balanced on their shoulders. Although the carriers were not often big, strapping, weightlifting types, they were still able to tip the coal from their backs into the narrow coal cellars in the houses. 'Briquettes' were another popular fuel to arrive at the Maxwell Street Goods Depot. They were made of large particles of coal dust or dross, formed into small blocks, which were very useful on winter nights for banking up an open fire, since they burned for a considerable time and were more economical than coal. They were loaded, rather like bricks, onto small horse-drawn carts and sold up to the tenement windows with the street cry, 'Briquettes! . . . Eglin-ton Briquettes!' Unlike coal, which was in bags, briquettes were sold loose and had to be carried up the stair on a short wooden board with only rudimentary handgrips at each end.

A lively and noisy cargo to arrive at the goods yard was a flock of sheep which was collected by Mr Crosbie, a local shepherd, and driven along Maxwell Street, where some of the animals would elude the dogs and try to escape into the stairway entrances. They were then guided across Morning-side Road, with a lot less traffic then, and eventually up Braid Avenue to graze in a field at the end of Hermitage Drive, below the slopes of Blackford Hill.

However, my days of observing the bustle of Maxwell

Street from our front room window, or from other parts of Morningside while accompanying my mother as she went her messages, were soon to be curtailed as I was confronted by one of the laws of the land – compulsory education! When I began school in 1925, my mother was, however, in no danger of sitting in solitude and depression in a quiet house as my younger brother, Bill, would not join me at school for another few years.

I must confess that I did not look forward to attending school. It seemed to indicate the end of freedom; but there was no escape. On a late August morning in 1925 many mothers gathered at the large iron gates of South Morningside School holding their five-year-old future scholars by the hand. Then the dreaded moment came. The boys made their way, with their mothers on this first enrolment day, up the red-sandstone steps with their broad balustrades (which still remain), along the main passageway, and into a large classroom on the left. Details were noted for enrolment and for the class register. Meantime, the infant girls, most of whom were also taking their mothers' hands, entered by a separate doorway off the south playground. Many a maternal tear was shed on this first day. I, meantime, made friends with John Ramsay, our close friendship remaining until his premature death, in 1942, on active service as a sergeant-observer (Volunteer Reserve) in the Royal Air Force.

Eventually, all the new entrants were enrolled and settled in. My first teacher was a genteel lady, Miss Rennie, who lived in Morningside Drive. However much we had been made welcome, I began surveying the Colditz-like sturdy walls and large windows for a means of escape. My chance came at playtime. With a great throng in the playground, where pupils enjoyed their morning 'piece', dutifully placing their empty paper bags in large metal refuse containers, I decided to make a break for it. I quickly slipped out of the main gate and made off down Comiston Road at the double. There were no prison warders in sight, nor did any alarm bells ring. My mother, however, suffered severe shock on answering the door bell and finding the reluctant scholar standing on the doormat. I got short shrift. Why had I come home? Was I unwell? Based on the belief that school attendance was voluntary, I simply stated that 'I don't want to join!' Fortunately my tall and sturdy grandfather was in our house that morning. I still remember my small hand being held firmly in his very large one, as I was marched back up Comiston Road. In any case, the infants' school day ended at mid-day, so I was soon back home again. I don't recall a penalty for this early absenteeism. There was, however, nothing else for it but to conform.

Next day I and my fellow scholars gathered in the playground. Mr Caws, the much loved janitor in uniform and peaked cap, appeared on the stone stairway and brought us all to order with a loud 'Shun'. At this command, for some reason which I never understood, we all jumped up and down on the spot. In we marched from our playground class lines, along the corridor, and up the stairs to the various classrooms on the first and second floor, all in strict time to the piano played, appropriately, by Miss Gravely.

In my classroom there was no sign of handcuffs or leg irons. Most classrooms had the desks in rows, tiered upwards from the front to the back. Those who were a little slow in learning, or who did not pay attention, were seated in the front row under the teacher's eye. The teaching method, after a lesson had been presented in 'reading, writing and arithmetic' or other subjects, was for the class to be questioned either at random or by a systematic progression, usually starting at the front row. For those who answered well, a regular reward was a sweet, often a wrapped mint lump from a bag in the teacher's desk. I did not receive a great many of those! Perhaps I was too often involved in pranks such as bouncing a golf ball from the top row down the steep steps to the front. The tawse, a leather belt or strap, was readily accessible in the teacher's desk, and regularly used.

A feature of the school year which appealed to me was the observing of the seasons: the growing of spring bulbs, decoration with autumn and winter leaves and berries, and holly at Christmas time. A Remembrance Day service was held every year in November at which the main hymn was always 'For All the Saints'. Those pupils who were members of The Boys' Brigade, the Scouts, the Guides or the Brownies proudly wore their uniforms on the 11th itself.

One weekly event, which meant more to me than academic achievement, was the appearance at the classroom door of one of the teachers, Mr Lowrie, who acted as the school football team manager. He was given a few minutes by the teacher to announce which boys in the class had been picked to wear South Morningside's blue and navy jerseys on the forthcoming Saturday. It was my week's finest hour if I had been chosen. We were due at one of Meggetland's many pitches at 9 a.m. on Saturday without fail. The school team did well in the Edinburgh primary league. A special honour was to be picked to play in a cup tie at Warriston – Edinburgh schools' Hampden – which had very fine turf. Several South Morningside boys, later through the 55th St Matthew's Boys' Brigade team, graduated to junior and professional football. A number might have made a name in Scottish football but, like many other former pupils, never returned from the Second World War. This included Ian Miller who lived in Comiston Road.

The culmination of school days at South Morningside

was the now much-maligned 'Quali' or Qualifying Examination which was taken at the age of eleven. Success, or otherwise, led to Boroughmuir Senior Secondary School (now Boroughmuir High School) in Viewforth, Darroch in Upper Gilmore Place, or Tynecastle in McLeod Street. By some minor miracle I was admitted to Boroughmuir. Other pupils went on to Edinburgh fee-paying schools such as George Watson's and Heriot's.

Boroughmuir and Broughton, two of Edinburgh's principal senior secondary schools, had very good reputations. They produced many pupils who made their mark academically in the professions, in Edinburgh city life and beyond, and also in the world of sport. I journeyed to Boroughmuir on foot, with others from Morningside, tending to walk and half-run to ensure that we arrived at 9 a.m. Many of us hurried home for lunch, although there was a perfectly good cafeteria on the top floor of the school.

To the disappointment of the sports lovers amongst us, Boroughmuir did not go in for football, and indeed many of us thought, perhaps unfairly, that those who played rugby were favoured by the gym teacher. Many pupils played for Boys' Brigade football teams on a Saturday afternoon and concerned mothers did not wish their boys to play rugby in the morning and also football in the afternoon. The gym teacher did not like this loyalty to The Boys' Brigade. On Fridays, if a rugby player was feeling unwell he was excused gym, but afternoon football players were not given the same consideration. Rather ironically, a lot of football was played in the playground at lunch time, right up until the last minute, with a frantic dash to get into the classroom in time for the next period. Playground football sessions, with the proverbial 'tanner' rubber ball, produced a number of future Edinburgh professionals.

While I had gradually adapted to life at South Morningside, I found myself having to begin this process again at Boroughmuir. Although a few members of my first-year class had also come from Morningside, the vast majority had come from different parts of Edinburgh. I found this somewhat off-putting. New friendships had to be made, and the range of subjects and the teaching methods were very different from South Morningside. Looking back, I wish that after the qualifying examination we had continued into secondary education in our local school. This, of course, was not possible but, in any case, it was probably beneficial, psychologically, and in the growing-up process, to have studied with new faces. The size of Boroughmuir also had to be reckoned with, as its roll of probably 1500 pupils was much greater than at South Morningside.

My father and mother believed that school provided only part of a child's education. School equipped one for life but did not claim to teach what life was about. At an early age, I was sent to Sunday School at Braid Church and this continued in parallel with secondary education. I have always been most grateful that my parents held such views and acted upon them. They profoundly helped and affected me. As a result of attendance at Sunday School, and later at the 55th Company of The Boys' Brigade Bible Class on Sunday mornings in St Matthew's (now Cluny) Church Hall, we gained quite substantial knowledge of the Bible at a relatively early age.

Sunday School classes were well attended, and included many of my friends from school. I suppose the highlights, socially, were the Sunday School picnic and the Christmas dance. The former was often held at the great mansion of Newhailes, near Musselburgh. After the sports programme was finished, everyone received a picnic paper bag, or cardboard box, containing a Scotch pie and buns, which were washed down with lemonade or cola, either straight from the bottle or from our own mug. The first week in June seemed to be the most popular time for picnics, presumably on the assumption that the weather would be good.

The Sunday School Christmas Dance was held in Braid Church's large hall which was copiously decorated to create a real Christmas atmosphere. I vividly recall, with my young fellow partygoers, looking out, rather nervously, from the boys' cloakroom over to the girls' room, each of us pushing the other out into the hall. The smell of perfume from the girls' cloakroom was overwhelming. I don't recall, in those early days, any fumes of after-shave emanating from the boys' quarters!

TWO

Some Work and Some Play

IN THE 1930s, at the time of the great economic depression and widespread unemployment, many Morningside families, as elsewhere, suffered hardship. Whatever the hardships, birthday or Christmas presents were, somehow, always provided, but far removed from the expensive gifts which many children receive today. Many presents from Santa Claus were secretly bought second-hand from press advertisements, and then repainted or made to look like new.

In the first years of secondary school, pocket money, modest enough, could always be supplemented with 'a nice little earner' by joining the district's great army of part-time delivery boys. Girls were also employed, but not so frequently in the early morning when it was still dark. I signed on at the age of twelve with McIntosh's Dairy, originally at No. 370 Morningside Road and then at No. 412 nearer to Morningside Station. One round which I had, starting at 6 a.m., took me via Morningside Drive to the streets around Plewlands and Craiglea Drive, finishing at Greenbank farmhouse where the Boa family lived. Delivery of milk to the farm became necessary after it ceased its own milk production in 1933. Another round was by Cluny Avenue and Cluny Gardens, almost to the Blackford Pond side gates at the bottom of Midmar Drive. This round was very convenient as it allowed me to visit, briefly, the family allotment facing Blackford Hill, where my father had given me a sizeable piece of ground on which I grew various vegetables. Some of these I sold at very nominal prices to neighbours in

Maxwell Street. Another small source of income was obtained by chopping up empty wooden boxes from local shops and selling bundles of firewood to housewives in Maxwell Street in the days when open coal fires were commonplace.

The milk was brought to McIntosh's, and to other local dairies, from outlying farms, in very large churns, which were lifted down from the small lorries and rolled on their lower rim into the shop. The milk was then emptied into large porcelain containers, each holding perhaps ten gallons, perched on the front counter. It was then poured into bottles, or pitchers, using a small metal, jug-like dispenser with a spout. Plain cardboard discs without tabs were then pressed, by hand, into the neck of the filled bottle. The days of aluminium caps, put on by machinery in factories to avoid hand contact, were a long way off. Pitchers holding two pints were also filled in this way. If there was a shortage of bottles any morning, empties had to be collected from the nearest tenement flat doors, where they had been put out the previous evening, before we began our round. They were simply rinsed in either hot or cold water in the back room of the dairy and then refilled with milk.

Milk was frequently delivered to the big houses in the Cluny, Midmar and Braid area in the two-pint pitchers. The delivery boy rang the bell at the kitchen door and a servant took in the pitcher, the sound of the milk gurgling into a large, unseen jug clearly heard from our lowly position on the doormat. Cream, single or double, in very small pitchers with large handles, was also supplied. Butter, and other dairy products, if ordered, were delivered on certain days of the week.

Mr McIntosh kept his fleet of two- and four-wheeled wooden and shafted barrows in little stone-covered cellars underneath long flat flagstones in front of what is now

Morningside Post Office. This flagstoned top is referred to by Joseph Laing Waugh in his little classic book *Robbie Doo*. My close school friend and companion, John Ramsay, and I had an occasional 'little earner' when we had the after-school job of painting the wooden barrows a rather uninteresting brown colour. We obtained the paint from the drysalter, Weddell, once at No. 183 Morningside Road near the corner with Falcon Road West. In these days, the business of drysalter (defined by Chambers' dictionary as 'a dealer in dyes and gums') was usually combined with that of ironmonger.

There were, of course, other after-school jobs, some of which remain today. Many of my friends delivered morning rolls, usually from Torrance the famous Morningside family baker, or from St Cuthbert's Co-operative Society – more usually referred to as 'the store'. St Cuthbert's had several shops in Morningside Road: the baker was between Steel's Place and Falcon Road; and the grocer, butcher, greengrocer and chemist were between Morningside Park and Springvalley Gardens. Torrance was at the corner of Comiston Road and Belhaven Terrace, and later at No. 356, opposite present-day Morningside Post Office, its speciality being Kettledrum Shortbread. Morning rolls and popular bran scones, newly baked and still warm, were delivered in paper bags in a large wicker basket with a shoulder handle. There was a special skill in delivering morning rolls, practised at many of the large villas in the area. In the morning, the large outer, wooden door was usually open, revealing an often tiled inner vestibule before the glass panelled inner door. To save ringing the door bell (at least that was the theory!) the bag of rolls, by the application of an acquired skill, could be thrown carefully from the street gate to land just in front of the glass panelled door, provided the throw was low enough. If not, of course, there was possible disaster. The bag could burst, scattering the rolls everywhere, or the glass panel could be in need of repair! Fortunately, such incidents were rare. One could sense that something had gone wrong if a customer was seen, in a rather agitated state, having a word with the shop manager. The delivery boy was duly summoned to explain himself but the skill was still widely practised.

Newspaper delivery, unlike milk delivery, had the advantage that the paper, correctly folded with the fold facing the door to prevent it opening in flight, could land safely at the inner doorway. In tenements, of course, the paper was put through the letter box or laid on the doormat. Some after-school messengers worked for grocers or butchers, both of which provided an attractive bicycle with a holder for a basket in front of the handle bars. Many shops would readily deliver a single item if a request was received by telephone. The store butcher sent a boy round in the early morning who rang the bells at the foot of the tenement stair and shouted 'Butcher!' As the boy showed no inclination to climb to the top flat, the housewife felt obliged to call her order over the banister. This could be a delicate operation – after all, it was not everyone, especially in Morningside, who wanted the neighbours to know that only a quarter of a pound of mince was being ordered to feed a family of four.

A welcome feature of Christmas was the often generous tips or gratuities given to the messengers. An envelope could be left with the tip under an empty milk bottle, but for paper boys and morning rolls boys Christmas saw an increase in doorbell-ringing, which did not usually take place at other times of the year. Often Christmas tips were handed into the shop by the customer.

Such, then, were the many ways of supplementing pocket money, but there were families where the whole of a message boy's weekly wage, frequently 3/6d (17.5p), was handed over to parents, and some handed back in return. Changed days! However, it was not all work and no play: for the most part, there was plenty of time for leisure activities.

Edinburgh has a rich heritage of street games, many of which are described in fascinating detail by former school teacher, James T. R. Ritchie in his valuable archival study *The Singing Street*, published in 1964, which was made into a film. This was followed by *Golden City* in 1965 which was reprinted by Mercat Press of Edinburgh in 1999. Most games were for boys or for girls but the lines of demarcation were by no means strict, and mixed teams were quite common.

Unless one was committed to an after-school newspaper delivery round, the late afternoon was a fairly carefree time. Soon after arriving home from school and perhaps while still enjoying a brief snack, the door bell would ring. There was a chum on the doormat: 'Is Charlie coming out to play?' Still chewing, and with all thoughts of homework cast aside, school uniform was discarded in favour of old clothes and shoes. We ran quickly downstairs and into the street where many others were already gathering. Hopefully, someone would have a 'tanner' rubber ball. Sides were picked and battle commenced, using the street lampposts and adjacent garden railings as goal posts. Play was frequently interrupted, usually by a horse and cart or lorry passing along Maxwell Street from the goods yard. If a sharp-eyed player spotted a policeman passing at the end of the street on Morningside Road, the players would disappear with practised speed into the various tenement doorways until all was clear. However, if we did not move quickly enough, the policeman invaded the pitch and several names were recorded in the dreaded little black notebook. Real names were not always given but he probably

knew everyone's name in any case. There was always the
fear of a court appearance but this never materialised:
maybe the policeman was a football enthusiast! Those
who had an after-school delivery round joined in the game
later. When a latecomer arrived, he was asked if he wanted
to be a 'cock' or a 'hen' to determine which of the two teams
he was to play for.

The game was also played with the large ball which we
called 'the full sizer'. The internal rubber bladder was
blown up with the use of a bicycle pump, and the leather
cover laced up. Favourite pitches were a patch of waste-
ground at Plewlands, near Plewlands Avenue and the sheep
pens at the Braid Hills, entered from Braid Hills Drive. On
the Braid Hills there were no touch lines, which meant that
a player could take the ball quite a distance up the surrounding slope whilst being pursued by an opponent.
Scores were high as full time was dictated only by the
approach of darkness. After the game there was a welcome
drink of cold water from a tap at Braid Farm on the long
exhausting walk home.

Most notable among these early, hardy, hill-climbing
players were Archie Proudfoot, who later played for East
Fife, and Tommy McKenzie of Jordan Lane, 'Big Toma', a
former pupil of South Morningside School, who later
became a stalwart in the Heart of Midlothian defence.
Another Hearts player was outside left-winger 'Tiddler'
Murray who did not graduate at the Braids but who
had a general shop at the west corner of Bruce Street
and Balcarres Street. Such was our reverence for professional players that if we learned that Murray was in his
shop we went along Balcarres Street and, crouching down
so as not to be seen, crossed back and forth at his shop
door in the hope of catching a glimpse of our hero. 'There
he is', we whispered, gazing in awe. Hibs supporters, of

course, were not interested and mocked the Hearts wor-shippers.

One skill, developed in Maxwell Street football and which was not required on the larger pitch, was the ability to prevent the small ball from being constantly kicked over the railings into the tidy little gardens, many of which displayed fine flowers and shrubs and were rather vulner-able. When the ball did go over, the player who had kicked it had to scale the spiked railings to get it back, hoping to be in and out before the owner appeared at the window angrily shaking a fist.

In addition to football and occasional cricket, there was an informal athletics contest held annually between Max-well Street and Millar Crescent. The events included the 100 yards, 220 yards and the mile, which consisted of an almost infinite number of laps of Maxwell Street. The marathon seemed to be limitless: across the railway footbridge, along Balcarres Street, up Plewlands Terrace, down Morningside Drive and back over the railway footbridge – for those who survived! The high and long jumps were popular but some of the other field events required some improvisation, including the use of a long cane as a javelin and a large heavy stone for putting the weight. Jim Howden, of Millar Crescent, who was especially good at the 'hop, step and jump', went on to appear in athletics contests in various parts of Scotland, and was a champion several times. It is not on record if any Olympic records were ever broken!

Another popular game was 'Cuddie Loups' which we always believed had been brought to Morningside by the Armour family from their home town of Campbeltown where the game was played by fisher lads on the sea front. Cuddie Loups took its name from the basic idea of one team 'louping', or leaping, onto the backs of the other team who were the 'cuddies' or donkeys. One team of five or six players bent over, in a line, beside their leader, usually against garden railings, while the other team, of equal number, ran one after the other, and jumped as far as they could onto the bent backs of the cuddies. There was then a count up to ten during which the loupers tried to collapse the cuddies, in which event the cuddies had to remain cuddies for the next game. If the loupers failed to collapse the cuddies, then it was the loupers' turn to be the cuddies.

One additional useful purpose which the coal trucks in the railway goods yards served, was to supply us with thick grease from containers fitted near the trucks' heavy wheels which we used to lubricate the wheels of our guiders. These were considered by the older generation to be a hazardous feature of the Morningside streets in summer. Guiders were constructed from empty wooden boxes begged from local shops and fitted with old pram or go-car wheels, complete with axles, which were fixed by large metal staples to narrow pieces of wood under the bodywork. Sometimes wooden wheels were fixed to wooden axles which required a lot of grease to reduce the friction. The front axle was designed to swivel on another piece of wood which pro-truded from the front of the guider. Rudimentary steering was achieved with the use of a rope attached to the front axle. More ambitious, and demanding real craftsmanship, were the guiders made from very large and long empty wooden egg boxes, which had a closed-in bonnet for covered leg space and concealed ropes, or a wheel, for steering. Such young enthusiasts, with design skill and daring, might have graduated to Formula One Racing! In addition to the guiders, one could raise a good speed with a scooter, or, of course (with luck at Christmas or at a birthday) a tricycle or the smallest size of bicycle usually known as a fairy cycle. Another popular pastime was to drive a large wooden hoop with a stick; or similarly an old

I was born on 16 June 1920 in an area basement flat at No. 9 Glengyle Terrace within the sound of the great bell which hangs in Pilkington's Barclay Church. *Photograph by Phil Seale*

The interior of the former McCrie Roxburgh United Free Church in Davie Street, *c.* 1915, where my mother and father sang in the choir and where I was baptised. *Courtesy of the author*

My mother, Johan (Joey) Smith, née Ranken, photographed at Campbell Harper's studio in Leith when she was twenty-four years of age.
Courtesy of W. R. Smith

My father, Charles J. Smith, also photographed at Campbell Harper's
studio in Leith when he was twenty-four years of age.
Courtesy of W. R. Smith

My paternal grandparents, Charles James Smith and his wife, Isabella, née McWatters. *Courtesy of W. R. Smith*

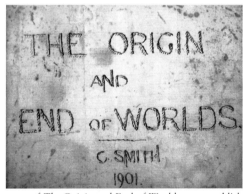

The title page of *The Origin and End of Worlds*, an unpublished script written in 1901 by my grandfather, Charles James Smith. *Photograph by W. R. Smith*

Three generations of the Ranken family, *c.* 1900. My maternal grandfather, William Ranken, with his mother Margaret Forrest Ranken, née Howden, on the left and his wife Sarah Jane Ranken, née Elliot on the right. The girl in the centre is my mother and the infant is my uncle John who was killed in the First World War. *Courtesy of W. R. Smith*

The Eagle Public House in Shepherdess Walk, near Taplow Street, London in 1975 referred to in the famous rhyme *Pop goes the Weasel*. My father lived for a short while in Taplow Street as a boy at the end of the nineteenth century. *Photograph by W. R. Smith*

A class of forty-six on the steps of the north entrance to South Morningside School in 1925. The teacher, Miss Rennie, is on the left and I am on the extreme right of the second back row in front of the student teacher, Miss Margaret Simpson. *Courtesy of Mrs Margaret McGregor, née Macpherson, who also appears in the picture fifth from the left in the middle row*

Boroughmuir School opened in Warrender Park Crescent in 1904 and transferred to this building in Viewforth in 1914. I attended there from 1932 to 1934. *Courtesy of Malcolm Cant Publications*

Boroughmuir School, Viewforth, Edinb

Craiglea Dairy at No. 98 Comiston Road was run by Mr Peter McKay and his wife Mrs Jane McKay, née Muirhead, from 1930 to 1937. The photograph shows Mrs McKay, on the right, and her assistant in the shop, c. 1934. *Courtesy of Mrs Marion C. Wright, née McKay*

Torrance's baker and confectioner (famous for its Kettledrum shortbread) was on the corner of Comiston Road and Belhaven Terrace. The Kettledrum Tea Rooms were a popular venue for afternoon tea, lunches and also business meetings by various local organisations. The delivery boys can be seen with their baskets on the pavement outside the shop. *Courtesy of Malcolm Cant Publications*

A fleet of three home-made guiders is hardly sufficient to reduce the queue of young lads waiting 'patiently' in line. *Courtesy of The Scotsman Publications Ltd*

A wide variety of skipping games were played by girls, well into their teenage years, in every district of Edinburgh. *Photograph by Raymond Townsend. From* Golden City *by the late James T. R. Ritchie*

pram or go-car wheel with a wooden or metal stop in the hole. Roller skates were also popular although the skateboard era was still a long way off.

A game which required only a small capital outlay was marbles or 'bools'. These were of various sizes and made of clay, glass or steel. They were also known as 'chuckies' and 'dollickers'. A very large glass bool with a coloured glass centre piece was known as a 'cat's eye'. A 'plonker' was a bool which you used to strike the other bools. There was also a wide variety of games such as 'holie', 'stakie' and 'knickelie', the intricate rules and regulations being described in great detail by James T. R. Ritchie in *Golden City*. In practice, the rules tended to vary between different parts of the town and even within the same districts. Players were very proud of their collection which was built up gradually from their weekly pocket money. The marbles were usually kept in a small cloth bag closed with elastic at the top. In the present day of concern with hygiene, especially for children, some readers may be horrified to learn that many of the games with marbles were played in the pavement gutters when they were dry.

James T. R. Ritchie devotes a substantial part of *The Singing Street* and *Golden City* to games played by the girls. These were, for long, a feature of Morningside streets as in other parts of the city. The spacious diagonal corner outside Bennet's Bar, at the north corner of Maxwell Street and Morningside Road, was a popular place for 'peeries', small wooden tops with a pointed metal tip, which could have their flat top coloured to produce a pattern on spinning. A whip of string, leather or cord was used to strike the peerie and keep it birling. One particular model, with a mind of its own, was known as the 'window breaker'.

'Peevers' were also enjoyed by girls, the peever beds being marked out on the pavement either with chalk or mother's pipe clay which was normally used to whiten the outside doorsteps of main door houses. Apparently there were many variations of peevers but the boys never really got involved except, perhaps, to disrupt the game. An empty shoe polish tin was commonly used to be nudged into each square while hopping on one leg. 'Diabolo' was another popular and skilled girls' game. The egg-timer-shaped wooden piece was spun on string held between two wooden handles, then cast high into the air and caught on the string when it came down, and tossed up again.

While the boys were engaged in football, usually in the middle of Maxwell Street, or on one of their away pitches, the girls played at the goods yard end of the street. Boys were often allowed to join in. Of the games which I recall, three may bring back memories for my contemporaries who, I am sure, will remember others. Many of these games revolved around the idea of the participants taking it in turn to be het (it or out). In 'Red Lights', the player who was het faced the garden railings with the other children lined up across the street. The het player counted silently up to ten, during which time the other players hurried across to reach the den before she suddenly turned round and shouted 'Red Lights'. The het player was allowed to decide the speed at which she counted so as to maintain the element of surprise. Everyone who was caught moving after she had finished counting and had turned round had their name called out and had to go back to the other side of the road. Eventually one of the players managed to reach the den while the het girl was still counting. That player then became the het player, and so on.

'Kick the Can' involved an empty can which was thrown away along the street. The het player retrieved the can and placed it in a chalked circle, or den, hiding her eyes and counting aloud up to ten. The other players then hid and

were sought by the het player after she had stopped counting. When the het player spied someone, she would call out
her name, and sometimes her location if the call was likely
to be challenged. Both the het player and the person spied
then ran back to the den in an effort to kick the can first,
and shout 'Kick the Can'.

A game with quite ancient origins was 'A-leevoy' or
variations on this name. The player who was het, and
based in the den, came out to try and catch the other
players. All those caught were placed in the den, but could
be released by a free player who stealthily crept up without
the het player noticing. By placing one foot in the den, and
shouting 'A-leevoy', a free player could release all the
prisoners.

'Rounders', a team game played by boys and girls, was
rather like American baseball, using a tennis or small rubber
ball bowled to the batsman wielding a broken-off broom
handle or similar stick. The batsman, having made a good
strike, immediately ran round a square pitch of four stations
as quickly as possible, hoping to reach the base before the
ball was quickly returned to catch him or her out. In more
involved versions of the game, with a greater number of
children in each team, it was permissible for a batsman to
take refuge at one of the intermediate stations and complete
the rounder on the strength of the next batsman's strike.

Very many forms of skipping were popular and required
practice and skill. It was in relation to these that many of the
rhymes recorded in *The Singing Street* were sung. Perhaps
the best known of the singing rhymes was:

> She is handsome, she is pretty,
> She is the girl from the Golden City.

The girl skipping kept in time to the words. It has never
been clear as to where 'The Golden City' was, but one

version of the rhyme refers to 'Belfast City'. Another rhyme was:

> I call in my very best friend,
> And that is Lynda Phillips
> One, two, three . . .

The 'very best friend', Lynda Phillips, or whoever else was called, then joined in and both girls carried on skipping together. Yet a third rhyme was:

> Kings and Queens
> And partners two
> All dressed up
> in Royal blue.
>
> Stand at ease
> Bend your knees
> Salute to the east
> And bow to the west.

Such were some of the simple pleasures of the day, enjoyed by girls of all ages even up to the age of going to secondary school.

THREE

The Boys' Brigade

VALUABLE RELIGIOUS education was provided by the many well-attended local Sunday schools in and around Morningside. This emphasis on religious training was also an important feature of The Boys' Brigade which held a mandatory bible class on Sunday mornings.

The 55th St Matthew's Company, which I joined aged twelve, was a great source of comradeship and enjoyable activities, apart from its provision of instruction and training in many subjects of interest and value. Friday was drill parade night. Uniform was worn, which in my day included a leather belt which had to be kept shining, as did the metal buckle bearing the B.B. motif of Anchor and Cross. The white haversack, which was worn from the right shoulder to the left hip, was kept immaculate, usually through being starched by our mothers. The black pill box, with chin strap and double line of white cording around it, was rather difficult to keep white with Blanco, which, when applied moist, had a habit of marking the dark surround. Badges were worn on important parades, and it was our aim to add to our uniform with lance corporal's, corporal's and sergeant's stripes (another task for the Blanco!) which were worn between the elbow and shoulder on the right arm.

Bible class, held at 10 a.m. on Sunday mornings, was considered to be the core of the B.B.'s influence and training: in the 55th it was usually conducted by the assistant minister of St Matthew's. Between fifty and sixty boys attended in the large church hall where we sat in rows facing the speaker. There were hymns, including the specifically B.B. hymns, viz., 'Underneath the Banner' and 'Will Your Anchor Hold' . Then there was a short address which often dealt with the moral problems facing boys and the Christian way of acting. I think that most boys were influenced to some degree, particularly in later life, by what they learned at bible class.

A wide variety of activities was also provided during the week. Wednesday was P.T. or physical training night, which included gymnastics and was held in the basement gymnasium of South Morningside School. Certainly it was an evening to keep fit, at which the skilful swinging of Indian clubs was also taught. Another evening, for those interested in more physical activity, was devoted to cross-country running, which entailed running from the school, in all weathers, through the Braidburn Valley Park and back to the gym. For several years, this form of athletics, now more popular in various city marathons, was in the capable hands of St Matthew's assistant minister, the Rev. Bill Whalley. Who better to coach us than he, a cross-country runner and former half mile (800 metres) champion of Scotland. The 55th Company entered a team each year in the Edinburgh Battalion Cross Country Championship and a few of us gained reasonable places. I had the honour of winning the Bill Whalley Cup in 1937, the year after he had donated it to the Company. The 55th also won the Battalion team event on nine occasions (including six consecutive years) from 1944.

I was one of the many boys who attended the first aid class which led to a badge in this subject. For some strange reason it was always referred to, informally, as the ambulance class. Our tutor was the popular, and very competent, Lieutenant Douglas Sutherland. The lectures and demonstrations were held in the small room immediately on the left on entry to the church hall. During one class, large illustrations of the skeleton, the digestive system, the brain and other areas, graced the walls. Douglas Sutherland was an excellent and enthusiastic teacher which probably accounted for the fact that in my fourth year of the class I won the Battalion Shield, awarded for written and practical examinations.

There was first a written examination in first aid. Depending upon the mark obtained, a number of candidates for the Battalion Shield were selected for a very demanding practical examination of simulated accident cases or of medical conditions. We were told that the 'acting' patient had been discovered lying on the floor unconscious, and we were asked to diagnose the cause of collapse and say what first aid should be given. This involved examining the patient for any visible injuries, taking the pulse rate and observing the state of breathing. I recall that my test case was of an epileptic fit which had to be identified from various signs and then treatment given before the arrival of a doctor. The practical steps were taken and the case was discussed with Dr McLaren, a small, pleasant man with a busy general practice in Lauriston Place.

A memorable occasion, in 1933, was the celebration of the Jubilee of the foundation of The Boys' Brigade, when the 55th Company joined other companies from every part of Scotland in a great parade in Queen's Park, Glasgow, the city where Sir William Smith founded the first company in 1883. Another celebration, held in Edinburgh in 1936, was the staging of *Edinburgh Rock* in the King's Theatre, each company providing amateur actors for the many scenes which told the history of the Edinburgh Battalion's fifty years through narrative and music. The dressing rooms for this great theatrical occasion were the halls of nearby Barclay Church.

Behind the scenes at the Barclay Church was a lively

affair. I remember the boys, who had been made up to play female parts, 'flirting' with the other boys! Many of us were given a brownish complexion, made up from a cocoa mixture, which, after the show, was removed with some difficulty by applying coconut oil. It was all very messy.

The company football team played a notable part in the Edinburgh Boys' Brigade League. I had the privilege to play for the Edinburgh Battalion against Leith and Stirling, and as a substitute against Glasgow, but higher Scottish football circles, alas, did not pursue me. In the 55th Company, Ian Miller was quite outstanding, and played for the Edinburgh Battalion team against other Battalion teams outside Edinburgh. Ian and his brother, Hector, also a 55th member, among many others, did not return from the Second World War.

A special feature of the B.B. year was the Annual Display and presentation of prizes and badges, held in May in the church hall, which was always packed with parents and families. Perhaps these were especially enjoyable for mothers, who took great pride in having been behind the scenes for their boys during the year, ironing haversacks, pressing trousers and giving a wakening call on Sunday mornings. The Display was good entertainment, and included precariously-built human pyramids, Indian club swingers and frequently a musical item composed and produced by Douglas Sutherland. Winners of badges and other awards were greeted with thunderous applause.

The annual camps, in proper bell tents, were happy occasions, with not a few opportunities for character formation. I especially recall the camp at Skateraw, near Dunbar, and a Battalion camp at Kinbuck, near Dunblane. Organising a camp for around thirty boys was quite a task. The advance party, of say two officers and six senior boys, left the church hall at Cluny Gardens in a small lorry carrying the basic equipment. This included six or more bell tents, a marquee for meals, heavy cooking utensils, supplies for the special medical tent, stakes and canvas for erecting latrines, and many other items. This advance party arrived at the camp site on the Friday evening to erect the tents and make general preparations. I well remember one occasion at Skateraw when it was so stormy and was raining so hard, we were prevented from erecting the tents the first night, and after spending the night on the floor of the lifeboat station, we got the marquee and tents up only just in time for the arrival of the Company in the early afternoon.

Each morning, we were awakened at an early hour, either by a bugler playing reveille or by a piper marching round each of the tents in turn. On the Sunday morning the Company usually paraded to the local church. I recall marching a considerable distance from Skateraw to Innerwick, the officers and boys being led by the pipe band whose repertoire, on that occasion, was sorely stretched by the time we got to the church.

Camp food was prepared on a large open fire by a professional cook. Breakfast, and other meals, were served in the marquee. For breakfast, porridge was ladled out by boys at each of the wooden trestle tables. We brought our own plates from home which were usually tin, or Bakelite in the days before plastic. Washing up afterwards was done in basins using water which was neither very hot, nor very soapy. After breakfast, one of the officers took tent inspection for which all blankets had to be neatly folded and laid out with canvas kit bags outside the tent doors.

Visitors' day, on the Wednesday, brought many parents, keenly welcomed by the home-sick and the impecunious, in equal measure. My recollection is that most boys were eager to have their funds replenished for spending at the camp tuck shop. At the end of the week, the Friday night 'Beano', with a special menu of sweet things and plenty of soft drinks, was the Grand Finale, before we struck camp and headed for home the next day.

When the company pipe band was formed in 1932, I joined as a piper. We were tutored by Army Pipe Major Stark in a classroom in South Morningside School. The first lesson with the chanter was to learn how to cover, effectively, the seven finger holes on the front and the hole for the left thumb at the back. There were simple instruction manuals giving the notation of the various tunes. Among the first we learned were the slow march 'Skye Boat Song', then 'Kenmure's Up and Awa' and 'Scotland the Brave'. Transferring our playing of the chanter to the bagpipes required more tuition and considerable skill. Keeping the three drones on the left shoulder, without allowing them to slip off, took not a little practice. The tartan-covered bag needed to be kept full of air, at an even pressure, to ensure that the drones were kept going, and the tune sounded on the chanter without interruption. The drones, one bass and two tenor, each contained a large cane reed which could be tuned to the chanter by twirling the ivory-ended stem of the drone. Quite a lot of time was spent before a performance ensuring that the pipes were in tune. Each drone could be tuned separately by cutting off the air supply to the other two. The air supply was stopped by tapping the upper end of the drone and then reintroduced by flicking the finger across the same outlet. Unlike instruments in a brass band, which have a fixture, or marching lyre as it is called, to hold the music, the bagpipes do not have such a device. The fingering for the tunes must, therefore, be committed to memory.

Drumming is quite a separate skill which also requires close concentration in training. A pipe band has three types of drum. Firstly, there is the bass or big drum which sets the beat for marching and signals the imminent end of the bagpipes playing by striking a loud double beat. Then there is the much smaller side or snare drum which provides the very characteristic ratatat-tat sound. Finally, some bands also have tenor drums, with the drummers exhibiting impressive artistry and skill in the swinging of the tasselled sticks.

After learning how to play the bagpipes or the drums, the next thing to master was how to play while marching and counter-marching, keeping to the beat, and maintaining one's position in line. I recall that we had six pipers, led by the pipe major on the left who was the leader of the band and who gave the commands. Three side drums and a bass drum were the norm for the average B.B. pipe band. There was much to learn.

Boys from all parts of Morningside, especially Balcarres Street, provided a rich source of talent from various social backgrounds; the basis of many friendships, still treasured today. The lives of many were shaped by their membership and comradeship enjoyed on and off parade.

I can never give too much praise and appreciation for the dedication and sacrifice of spare time by officers both then and now. Those who, in my young impressionable mind, earned a kind of immortality were: Tom Taylor, the popular Captain; Lt. Jimmy Moyes, who commanded us meticulously for the annual Battalion Drill Cup; Lt. Archie Paul, no mean football player and team manager; Lt. Douglas Sutherland, of wide-ranging talents, but at his best when, pointer in hand, he took us through the intricacies of the skeleton on the wall chart; Lt. Frank Somerfield, company treasurer, of quiet nature but always there for us; and Sam Gannon who kept us fit on Wednesday evenings.

I am proud to record that love for, and dedication to, the B.B. was the mainstay of my father's life, from his early days in the 3rd Mayfield and Gifford Park Company, to serving later as acting captain of the 55th during the years of the Second World War. Well into his eighties, my father, as overseas secretary of the Ex-members' Association, regularly corresponded with 'old boys' throughout the world. My brother, Bill, worthily maintained our father's devotion by holding the captaincy from 1950 to 1960, during which time he took on various additional duties. These included the very onerous job of production manager of the highly successful show *Scotland the Brave* staged in the Empire Theatre in Edinburgh in 1954 to mark the centenary of the birth of Sir William Smith, founder of The Boys' Brigade.

The essential feature of The Boys' Brigade was, and still is, its link with the church and the Sunday bible class as a preparation for church membership. In expressing gratitude for my years in the 55th, I must include a special tribute to the Rev. Bill Whalley. In our training for cross-country running, he not only challenged us with the one-time motto of Edinburgh University Cross Country team 'Run till your guts hing oot', but also had a profound and lasting influence on my own spiritual life. Sadly, while giving a Good Friday sermon as a visiting minister in a United Free Church in Ayr, he had just quoted the words of the Gospel narrative 'It is finished' when he collapsed from a heart attack. He died soon after on 10th July 1981.

It is only now, in writing this autobiography, that I have been able to study records relating to Bill Whalley's achievements in the world of sport. When he took over training us in cross-country running in the 1930s, we had a vague idea that he, himself, had won several Scottish Amateur Athletic championships. Recently I discovered from various issues of the Edinburgh University publication, *The Student*, that Whalley had been an athlete of considerable ability. He participated in Edinburgh University Athletics Club meetings at Myreside and, as a representative of the club, had many successes in the Scottish inter-university contests, notably in the half mile and the mile. He ran with Eric Liddell of *Chariots of Fire* fame. He also had wins in various Open Scottish Championships and Edinburgh University's Hares and Hounds races.

A race of particular interest, especially to people in Edinburgh, was the Arthur's Seat Race, which began at what was then the Men's Union in Park Place beside the McEwan Hall. Having run from Park Place to the base of the climb in Holyrood Park, the runners had the option to ascend either by the 'Cat's Neck' or the 'Gutted Haddie', both of which had the added hazard of loose stones or scree. After reaching the 'Lion's Head', it was downhill most of the way back to Park Place. Bill Whalley won this race four times in five years in the early to mid-1930s, his fastest time being 19 minutes, 47.6 seconds in 1933. This race must have been considered a severe challenge, as it was reported in 1923 that it would take place only if the Edinburgh Medical Officer of Health approved. Fortunately, he did so.

Years later, after I began work in the Medical School, one of my senior colleagues in the Bacteriology Department, who was the secretary of the then Edinburgh Eastern Harriers, invited me to join this club, where I trained for cross-country racing. Another feather in Bill Whalley's cap.

Unfortunately, it seems to me that today athletics has moved away from being motivated by love of the sport to the incentive of financial reward without which many stars would not compete.

FOUR

Home Life at Maxwell Street

OUR HOUSE in Maxwell Street was the same size as most houses in the street, although some were larger. The main room of the house was the kitchen-cum-living room which was of reasonable size, and had a bed recess, which was not always used. There was a small coal fireplace and mantelpiece, and a porcelain tub and sink at the window overlooking the back green. The smaller sink was in use every day for washing dishes etc., but the larger tub was only used for washing and steeping clothes. It was fitted with a wooden top or bunker, which was very handy for small boys to sit on while having their knees scrubbed after much street playing! Originally, water was heated from a small tank at the back of the fire but in later years an immersion heater was fitted. Next to the kitchen was a good-sized bedroom, with a small coal fireplace which was seldom used unless one of us was confined to bed by illness. The parlour, or front room, also had a coal fire and a fine black marble surround and mantelpiece. Here, too, there was a bed closet, entered from the parlour.

As in most parts of Edinburgh, the house was lit by gas, with the mantle fitted in a short bracket which could usually be swung out from the wall for use. As darkness fell, the gas would be lit using a match or long taper. Entering the house after dark was more difficult as there was no convenient electric light switch near the door. I vividly recall the procedure when we returned to the house after shopping or visiting. On entering the darkened hall, my mother, brother and I waited in the hall while my father boldly advanced into the kitchen where he lit a match and hastily turned on the gas at the bracket above the fireplace. There was a hiss and the distinctive strong smell of town gas, followed by a loud plop which signified ignition. To begin with, the light was very weak but, as the mantle warmed up, the darker corners of the room were also illuminated. The gas mantle, which I believe was made of asbestos, was very fragile, but if it was damaged or burned away with use, it could be replaced quite cheaply from the drysalters in Morningside Road.

Many of the back greens, used primarily for drying clothes, were nicely laid out with trees and colourful flower beds. They extended from the back wall of the tenement, northwards to a railing-enclosed lane, which joined another lane at the west end of Maxwell Street near the steep brae leading up to Millar Place. Where the two lanes met, there was an iron grating, below which we could hear, and using a torch see, the junction of the very weak Jordan Burn and the more powerful Comiston Burn. Little were we to know then, that many years later Bill was to produce an excellent film in which he traced the course of the two burns. The Jordan Burn rises at Craighouse Hill, runs under Myreside Road and along the boundary wall of the Royal Edinburgh Hospital to the end of Maxwell Street. It then goes under Morningside Road, between the present-day Post Office and the front lawn of Morningside Braid Church, and along the back of the houses on the south side of Jordan Lane and the north side of Nile Grove. From there it runs by Woodburn House, the Astley Ainslie Hospital, Blackford, Mayfield and Greenend before joining the Braid Burn and entering the sea at Portobello as the Figgate Burn.

In the 1930s, few people in Morningside, or indeed Edinburgh, possessed electric washing machines. There were some of a mechanical, handle-turning type, heated

underneath by a gas ring but there were certainly no spin
dryers. During the weekly washing, shirt or blouse cuffs,
collars, etc. were first rubbed with soap and water to
remove excess soiling, using a ribbed scrubbing board.
After washing, the clothes were then put through a hand
wringer (the Acme type was popular) which was fixed onto
the joint in the sink between the washing-up section and the
deeper washing tub. After the excess water had been pressed
out, my mother took the clothes down three flights of stairs
to the back green where each household had its own
clothes' ropes tied to heavy iron poles. There was some
amicable, and sometimes less amicable, protocol involved.
Monday was the commonest washing day, one traditional
reason being that there was sufficient of Sunday's lunch left
over to save cooking on washing day. However, on account
of the drying green's limited capacity, not all housewives
could do their washing on that day, which meant that a
weekly schedule had to be agreed. Usually the person who
had lived in the stair for the longest time got Monday. On
whatever day was allocated, the ladies of the stair would go
down early and hang out their ropes to book a place,
occasionally creating mild friction if someone put up too
much rope. At No. 3 Maxwell Street, and also in other
stairs, there were cellar-type wash-houses with a tub and a
boiler but I cannot recall these ever being used. Fitted to the
ceiling in the kitchen-cum-living room of our house was a
long pulley which our mother used either to air the clothes
or to dry them when the weather was too wet to put them
out in the back green.

    An alternative, or addition, to the weekly wash was to use
the bagwash services of St Cuthbert's Co-operative Society
or other local laundries, many of which were in the March-
mont area. Braid Laundry had a leaving and collection
service at No. 265 Morningside Road, which was even-

tually demolished, with the house above it, to make way for a succession of small supermarkets and later today's Post Office. The actual laundry, for long owned by the Brotherstone family, was where the Angle Snooker Club is now situated. Earlier, there had been a laundry, Shoolbreads, at No. 4 Jordan Lane, and others in Balcarres Street and today's Cuddy Lane. My recollection of the bagwash was of my mother packing clothes into a blue checked-pattern bag with an elastic closing top, tied with cord. The bag, on collection days, was carefully dropped from the landing of our second-floor flat, over the railings into the well of the stair below, after checking that there were neither people nor prams in the way. The gas lighting brackets, protruding from the landing below, had to be carefully avoided to ensure that the gas could still be lit in the evening, either by my mother or one of the neighbours, depending upon whose turn it was. These laundries also had a special collection service for starching stiff white collars which many men wore on a shirt of different colour, fixed with special studs.

Compared to today it may seem as though life at Maxwell Street was quite hard. In fact, I know that both my mother and father were very happy when they moved to Morningside where they began a long period of stability and moderate progress. Although my mother always appeared fulfilled in her role as a housewife, a mother and a good neighbour, there is no doubt that in earlier years she had passed up opportunities for her own advancement. When she was at Bristo School her headmaster asked her to consider training to be what was known as a monitor teacher before the days of lengthy college training. Unfortunately, her family circumstances prevented her from taking up this excellent idea. Some years later, but before she was married, another opportunity arose when she was employed in Blair's, the outfitters. After showing considerable promise in various aspects of window-dressing, her employer suggested that she would benefit greatly by visiting London to see how the big fashion shops arranged their window displays. I am sure she would have liked to go, but, alas, family circumstances prevented it.

Her loss, however, was later our gain. I remember that in summer my mother would take my brother and me and several pals to Swanston where we had a picnic of sandwiches and other treats. The kettle for the tea was boiled on a small fire of sticks in a suitable corner of a dry-stane dyke. At other times she would take us on the suburban line from Morningside to Portobello for a picnic on the beach and a visit to the funfair. Although she did not have a lot of time for her own activities, she was still able to attend Braid Church Guild every week and take her turn serving soup and snacks to needy men and women at the 'People's Palace' café in the Cowgate, run by the Church of Scotland.

My father also enjoyed living at Maxwell Street, particularly when his employment situation improved. After he lost his job when Parkinson-Cowan moved to Manchester he obtained a succession of temporary appointments including the Ministry of Labour Employment Exchange at Tollcross, and a spell as a reader's copyholder with *The Scotsman* newspaper. He entered a new and happy era in his life when he obtained a permanent post with Bertrams Sciennes who manufactured paper-making machinery. He became the firm's welfare officer which entailed many different duties: he visited sick employees; he assisted in the smooth operation of the busy staff canteen and also in the production of Bertram's staff magazine; and he took on responsibility for the firm's outdoor recreation centre at Meggetland which had a bowling green, tennis courts and facilities for the employees' children. Perhaps his greatest delight was organising Bertram's Christmas Children's Party.

The working day of the average Edinburgh man was seven to eight hours from Monday to Friday, and from 9.00 a.m. to 12 noon on a Saturday. The suburban railway, popular for travel to and from work in the city, journeyed from Morningside Road Station to Waverley in fourteen minutes, as well as taking Morningside's many Heart of Midlothian football supporters to Gorgie Station on Saturday afternoons.

Holidays for tradesmen or manual workers were normally during Trades week, traditionally the first full week in July. Some would also get the week after, but not all such workers had holidays with pay. This situation was to improve over the years through trade union negotiation.

Very few ordinary people went abroad. Unlike today, with low-priced package tours, it was cheaper to take holidays in Britain. There were, however, exceptions: employees of the two main rail companies, the London North Eastern and the London Midland & Scottish, were given free travel vouchers for their families, some even including European rail travel. For many people, a week, perhaps a fortnight, in the Highlands might be possible, spent in a modestly-priced boarding house. Fife seaside resorts were popular as were North Berwick and Dunbar. In an era when few families had cars, travel was by bus, or by train on a cheap excursion fare.

My father and mother had a long tradition of going on holiday to Rothesay on the Isle of Bute. In fact, such was their fondness of 'doon the water' that they would also take my brother and me on day trips to Rothesay on public holidays. This was quite an expedition. We set off on foot from Maxwell Street (I cannot recall ever by taxi) for

Merchiston Station, which lay between Slateford Road and
Bonaly Road (now renamed Harrison Gardens). Our route
was by the lane at the end of Maxwell Street and up into
Morningside Park, and eventually into Colinton Road. We
turned into Gillsland Road and down Harrison Road to
Merchiston Station. The train we aimed for on a public
holiday left at 6.25 a.m. from the former Caledonian
Station at the west end of Princes Street for Glasgow Central
Station. This meant leaving home just before 6.00 a.m. At
Glasgow Central the train normally left from Platform 13
for Wemyss Bay. There was then a short sea-crossing via
Innellan, round Toward Point to Rothesay, and we arrived
for lunch in one of the seaside resort's many restaurants or
cafés. The journey home was the exact reverse of the above.
A long but, to us, very enjoyable day. At least an annual
visit to Rothesay, even for just a day, has continued in the
family for over seventy years. 'Of a' the airts the wind can
blaw, I dearly lo'e the west', wrote Robert Burns. The Smith
family made these words their own! It was only in later
years, after my marriage and my daughters Barbara and
Pauline had included Italian and French in their Edinburgh
University degrees, that we spent many holidays in Italy and
France.

Probably on account of the few people travelling abroad,
and the absence of television cookery programmes, there
was little desire for continental or oriental food. People did
not dine out very frequently. Whilst out shopping, a visit to
the Balmoral Tearoom in Darling's shop on Princes Street,
or Patrick Thomson's on the North Bridge, was a real treat.
In the days when Patrick Thomson's still had balconies
overlooking the ground-floor area, a small orchestra played
while the clientèle had afternoon tea.

At home, I seem to recall that there was not quite the
same rush to be off to work as there is today. Nowadays

many people have only a quick cup of tea or coffee and no food before dashing out in the morning. In earlier days, most people made time for breakfast, often porridge, or a cereal, although not from a very wide variety. Many would have bacon and egg or scrambled egg on toast. Morning rolls were popular, and bran scones. Sunday morning was the occasion for a full fry-up consisting of bacon, egg, sausages, black pudding, fried bread and tomato. At lunch time, or as an evening meal, there would be stewing beef, mutton, mince or even steak as a treat. Cabbage, cauliflower, Brussels sprouts, carrots, turnips, peas and, of course, potatoes were regularly on the menu, fresh vegetables being preferred to tinned. A Scotch pie provided a quick snack. Steak pie, with pastry, in a proper pie dish, was a popular wedding meal. On Saturday mornings, of course, our diet was extended, with the help of pocket money, to a wide assortment of sweets, consumed without much thought for the consequences of tooth decay. Our favourites included: Golden Charm Caramels; McCowan's 'Highland Cream' toffee; Bull's Eyes; Sherbet Dabs and Cream Snowballs – all washed down with lemonade, cola or Sugarallie Water, a home-made solution concocted mainly from liquorice.

Before the era of refrigerators and freezers, very many housewives shopped daily. By far the majority of those from the tenements went to 'the Store', run by St Cuthbert's Co-operative Wholesale Society. In my day, the Store grocer, greengrocer, butcher and chemist were situated at Nos. 200–210 Morningside Road, immediately south of the junction with Springvalley Gardens. The baker and later the shoe shop were opposite at No. 193. I vividly recall the grocer's shop which had a bare wooden floor and two long forms for customers to sit on while waiting their turn. So many local women went regularly to the Store that, especially in the grocer's, their friends would notice if they were missing. Was she ill, perhaps, or did she have some domestic problem? Could one look in and be some help? It was a close-knit, caring community.

Before the age of ready-packaged items, commodities such as sugar, flour, lentils and peas were weighed out from large sacks, as required, and tipped into thick brown paper bags, the tops of which were neatly folded and tucked in by the person serving, usually with great speed and dexterity. Instead of being pre-packed, bacon was sliced on the rotating round-blade machine. Butter was taken from a large slab covered in muslin, then weighed and skilfully shaped by wooden butter pats before being packed in grease-proof paper. The Maypole Dairy and Buttercup Dairy in Morningside Road also specialised in fresh and salt butter.

The Store baker had certain unique features. Bread was known as plain, square pan or high pan and wrapped at the counter in thin brownish tissue paper. Frequently, if it had just been brought in from the delivery van, from St Cuthbert's bakery at High Riggs and later Gardner's Crescent, the bread might still be quite warm from the oven. Some customers liked this newly-baked loaf whilst others, including my mother, preferred what was known as cutting bread i.e. baked earlier in the day, and therefore easier to slice. Morning rolls, also directly from the bakehouse, were floury, hard fired, or buttery. The loaves and rolls were packed onto long wooden boards which the van driver skilfully balanced on a rubber ring on his head to bring them into the shop. Frequently, the price of a loaf involved a farthing in the change (roughly equivalent to one-tenth of 1p) and instead of this, one was sometimes given a small currant biscuit. Why this was done I do not know as farthings were still legal tender and part of the normal currency. Perhaps the shopkeeper was short of change.

The Store baker and grocer had a special, and, looking back, unique and fascinating system, designed to convey the customer's cash payment to the cashier at the back of the shop, and to return the correct change to the counter assistant. The assistant placed the money in the hollow centre of a large wooden ball, a little smaller than that used in bowls. This was then hoisted by a cord up an enclosed column to a little platform. From there, the ball ran by gravity along wooden rails and dropped down the column into a net on the cashier's desk. The ball was unscrewed, the money taken out with the payment slip, and the correct change sent back again in the ball on another rail sloping toward the shop counter. The ball was again opened and the customer given the change and receipted check. In certain large stores in the city, the money was placed in a tubular container which was put into a vacuum tube which conveyed it to the cashier's department by a quite circuitous journey, usually in another part of the shop.

Whether purchased from the Co-op store, or from one of the many other privately-owned grocers, bakers, fish-mongers or greengrocers, a certain amount of ingenuity was required to store perishable food at home, in the absence of refrigerators and freezers. Fish would be placed between two large plates to ensure a certain coolness. Many housewives stood milk bottles in a container of cold water or poured the milk into a jug covered by a muslin or open-mesh cloth, soaked in cold water. As the water evaporated, the milk was kept cool. Meat could be kept between two plates on top of a marble mantelpiece, without a fire on, of course. Some households had a small wooden box with a mesh front, hinged in such a way that it could be swung out from the kitchen window. Perishable food could thus be kept at outdoors temperature in this very basic refrigerator.

A great boon for families with a rather modest budget

was the Co-op Store Book. This enabled customers to make larger purchases in various Co-op shops, viz. clothing, household goods etc. by requesting that the purchase be entered in 'the book'. The amount due in the book could be cleared over a period. Books were given to shareholders who paid a minimum of £5.00 to join. Each shareholder had a unique number, memorised and never forgotten. Ours was 59875 which I still remember after all these years.

Another benefit of buying from the Co-op was the accumulation of the Dividend. In the 1930s, it probably amounted to about 1/9d (9p) in the pound. Dividend was paid out twice each year and, depending upon how much had been spent, could be a useful sum. The 'Divi', as it was always known, was collected at the Music Hall in the Assembly Rooms in George Street (or at the Co-op's own store in Bread Street). A long queue formed in Rose Street at the back entrance to the Assembly Rooms. Inside the hall, tables were laid out to group the customers alphabetically by surname. I recall one particular feature of the Rose Street queue was a man playing on a large saw with a violin bow, collecting a good many contributions until the queue moved in quickly and he could not keep up with his outstretched cloth cap. Many young people, in families who patronised the Store, would be told that they would get that long-requested new school blazer, sports jacket or suit off the Divi. 'Be patient!'

In my young days, long before the National Health Service, there was a form of free medical attention for those who paid contributions from their wages. When a person was off ill, they were referred to as being 'on the Panel', the expression, presumably, coming from the panel of doctors who operated the scheme. In these days, many home remedies were quite common. Many mothers were influenced by various cures and treatments in the popular weekly *People's Friend* which is still widely read. Alternative medicine in the form of various potions was available from Napier's, the Herbalist, at Bristo. There was something for most complaints: Lobelia Syrup for stubborn coughs; Syrup of Squills and ipecacuanha wine for coughs and sore throats; and cascara or Gregory's Mixture (a Morningside product) commonly given to children at the weekend to keep them 'regular'. Both the latter had a dreadful taste, never to be forgotten. There were lotions for acne, that timeless worry of teenagers. Flowers of Sulphur were also taken to keep one 'regular' and to 'clean the blood'. As a general tonic, perhaps after a spell in bed, the home medicine cabinet could provide Radio Malt (perhaps with cod liver oil), Scott's Emulsion and Parish's Chemical Food, which was not very good for the teeth.

Hallowe'en was a great time of celebration in most homes. Children made their own 'tattie bogles' or turnip lanterns (as they still do) by scooping out the flesh of the large turnip using a knife or spoon. Slit holes were cut out for the eyes, nose and mouth, the latter being specially carved to create jagged teeth. A small candle was inserted inside, on the base of the turnip, and lit. With the sliced-off top lid replaced, and a string attached for carrying, a quite eerie glow emanated from the tattie bogle. To add to the atmosphere, the house was often draped with orange and black crêpe paper. Guising was popular at Hallowe'en, when we dressed up as witches and wore masks. In my youth, the local shops did not sell the wide range of Hallowe'en novelties available today. Our guising dress and accessories had to be home-made. Children dooked for apples and nuts in most homes, with joint parties making for a crowded room, all queuing up for a turn to aim a mouth-held fork at a rosy apple swishing with others in a large tub. Nuts were dooked for by a large spoon held in the mouth, and a treacle-laden scone, on a string, was either tied to the pulley or whirled round a circle of kneeling, open-mouthed children, all trying to obtain a bite as the scone continued its elliptical path.

Before the parties began, we set out round the district in our disguise of masks and cloaks or whatever old clothes our mothers could provide. When a householder answered the door bell, there we were, four or five of us, with turnip lanterns lit. As the door opened, we broke into song:

> This is the night o' Hallowe'en
> All the witches to be seen
> Some o' them black
> And some o' them green
> This is the night of Hallowe'en.

This was then followed by at least a couple of lines of 'Please to help the guisers'. Quite a sum of money could be made touring the high tenements of our part of Morningside. This led to us spending our hard-won wealth on a real feast, sitting in at our local fish and chip shop, rather than being confined to our usual small bag of chips to carry out. In those far off days, Hallowe'en was very much the traditional Scottish occasion, unlike now when, in American fashion, a large, carved out pumpkin has tended to displace the turnip tattie bogle, and 'Trick or Treat' has replaced the singing of traditional songs. Nor was Hallowe'en confused and celebrated along with the imported English custom of Guy Fawkes night with its bonfires and fireworks. Our fireworks and bonfires were always on Victoria Day in May. During the previous week we spent a lot of time going round the neighbourhood collecting material which then had to be closely guarded against any incursions from rival gangs.

Of more widespread celebration, of course, were Christmas and New Year. Again many young people were seen in Morningside's streets and stairs and you would hear a line or two of 'Good King Wenceslas' or:

> The New Year's coming
> The pigs are getting fat
> Please to put a penny
> In the old man's hat
> If you haven't got a penny
> A ha'penny will do
> If you haven't got a ha'penny
> Then God bless you.

At New Year, first-footing was widespread amongst neighbours in the tenement stairs. The television programmes which now bring in the New Year were still to come. The radio was more common in relaying the stroke of midnight. A few minutes into the New Year, the door bell rang and it was a neighbour and family from one of the other houses in the stair. First-footers, bottle in hand, with a lively and warm greeting of 'Happy New Year', were welcomed in, with handshaking all round. The visitors always offered a drink from their bottle which was reciprocated by their hosts, followed by more greetings all round. A visit was then paid to first-foot the neighbour who had called. More drinks and more good wishes all round. This could lead to an informal party into the small hours with more drinks and perhaps a song or two. It was not unusual for dawn to be approaching before everyone departed for a late sleep. Many people walked to the Tron in the High Street to bring in the New Year there. There were, for many, quite strict conditions for first-footing. Everyone hoped that the first person to enter their house after midnight would be tall, dark and handsome. Traditionally, for good luck in the rest of the year, they would carry a piece of coal and another small gift, for the lady of the house. It was not unknown for people, especially the lady of the house, to attribute subsequent bad luck or misfortune to their first-foot having the wrong colour of hair or some other shortcoming.

Personally I preferred Christmas celebrations to New Year. One had the spirit of Christmas created at Sunday School, primary school and at The Boys' Brigade bible class by the Bible readings and carol singing. There was great excitement and anticipation on Christmas morning thinking about the presents left by Santa Claus, that is, until one of your friends thought that valour was the better part of discretion: 'It's not true, you know, there's no Santa Claus. It's your father!' I don't remember the world coming to an end at this disillusionment! From then on, perhaps we should just have hoped for a bit less or something not quite so expensive. Sometimes, of course, Santa Claus was caught in the act of filling stockings and laying wrapped presents beside the fireplace when we were still lying sleepless with excitement. Whatever gifts Santa laid before the fireplace, we could all be sure that our stockings would contain an apple, an orange and a bright coin among other goodies. It was also great fun to discover what other young friends had received on Christmas morning and Maxwell Street, as no doubt elsewhere in Morningside, was the scene of new or second-hand tricycles being proudly and happily ridden, with scooters or bikes for the older ones. Long before electric Christmas lights became commonplace, most houses had an unlit tree, although not always displayed in the window. In later years, when my family were living at No. 22 Jordan Lane, I used to set out with my son, Charles, to gather holly growing wild in various locations in Morningside.

A much-enjoyed feature of Christmas was to be taken to

visit the various bazaars in Princes Street and St Cuthbert's Co-op in Bread Street. We gazed in wonder and longing upon Meccano sets, Hornby model train sets and a host of toys which we would like Santa to have left at the fireplace on Christmas Eve. The shops, however, always had a genial, kindly Santa and a box of lucky dips. There was once a popular belief that when colds and sore throats were prevalent early in January, these had been contracted in the cold streets, en route from one quite warm bazaar to another.

The service and carols at Braid Church were always the centre of our Christmas at Maxwell Street. A happy and memorable feature of home at Maxwell Street was its hospitable and generous openness to relations and neighbours. The highlight of my parents' entertaining was their New Year family gathering, celebrated in the true Scottish tradition. Hogmanay might have been a late and lively night of first-footing but they were still up early on New Year's Day.

In the evening of 1 January many members of the family gathered at my parents' house in Maxwell Street. Seating was arranged round the extended kitchen table to allow about twenty guests to sit down to a four course meal. Planks of wood were placed between chairs to provide more places and folding chairs, stools and everything usable was set out. Some of the adults would be precariously perched on low seats, with their faces barely showing above the level of the table, which was always good for a laugh. When everyone was seated it was well-nigh impossible to leave the table or the room. Small children were propped up on cushions on dining-room chairs. Paper decorations and Christmas crackers at each place made for a truly festive and colourful scene. Everyone sported paper hats, and jokes from the crackers were read out across the table to laughter and more banter. Occasionally, the chat could suddenly become heated and serious: a feature of New Year's Day was the traditional local Derby game between Hearts and Hibs. One of my uncles was an ardent Hearts' fan who lived almost within sight of Tynecastle, and another uncle was an equally devoted Hibee. Sometimes they had been at the match, or if not, had listened to the commentary on the radio. There was the danger that whichever team won, the victorious uncle would taunt the other about his team's poor performance. Even a draw could lead to one being worked up over a disputed penalty or disallowed 'goal', with the inevitable comments on the referee's eyesight. My father adopted a neutral role, trying to keep things under control so as to ensure proper appreciation of my mother's cooking.

When the meal was over, we adjourned to the front room, or parlour, which was also festooned with paper decorations. After a short interval, and aided by wine, beer, tea, coffee or soft drinks, the games began. There was something for all ages. Singers held forth beside the piano, their repertoires and abilities ranging widely, but including many old favourites. Dancers took to the floor for everything from the Eightsome Reel and Dashing White Sergeant to the Samba. Neighbours below had been advised in advance in case they thought that they had been hit by an earthquake. They would join the fun with other neighbours as the night went on. My mother would dress up and enter the room to cheers and laughter. Even then, all was not over. Tea cups were brought from the kitchen, along with currant loaf and shortbread, and sweets for the young ones. Suddenly it was time to go: not by car, usually by the night bus, and only occasionally by taxi. We waved from the window as guests made their way into the street and into the night: the first of the New Year. All were wished well without any thought of what the New Year held in store. Those were the days.

The mood of the country changed dramatically, however, in 1939, when the crisis in Europe indicated that war was almost inevitable. My friend, John Ramsay, and I followed developments closely and discussed the deteriorating situation at great length. In the evenings after work we would meet and enjoy exploring the district. One of our favourite walks was along the path above Braid Burn Valley which is reached today by Fly Walk off Greenbank Crescent, where we would sit talking about the latest news of Europe. There were many public meetings held in the city at which the possibility of war was discussed. Speakers at the Mound attracted large audiences. One crowded meeting in the Central Hall at Tollcross was addressed by the Rev. Dr George MacLeod (later Lord MacLeod of Fuinary), minister of Govan Parish Church, and founder of the Iona Community. Dr MacLeod was a pacifist who maintained that a Christian could not take part in war, although this was not the official view of the Church of Scotland. After the meeting, John and I gathered in a group around Dr MacLeod, inviting him to clarify his views. Also strongly opposed to war was the Peace Pledge Union whose speakers addressed meetings at the Mound and in various halls throughout Edinburgh. On 3 September 1939, after Hitler's invasion of Poland, Britain declared war on Germany. The press headlines heralded imminent conscription and the many other implications of war.

On account of my work in the Medical School of Edinburgh University, I was in what was known as a reserved occupation and was never called up. My friend John, after much soul-searching concerning the morality of war, volunteered for the Royal Air Force as an air gunner where he gained the rank of Sergeant Observer. After training at various stations in England he took part in many Lancaster bombing raids over Germany. Tragically, on 1 October 1942, at Syerston in Nottinghamshire, his Lancaster bomber, on take off on a path-finding flight, developed a fault and crashed to the ground. He and the other members of the crew were killed instantly. John was laid to rest in the little picturesque cemetery at Lasswade with which his family had been associated. His funeral and interment were attended by several senior pilots of his squadron.

In Maxwell Street my father was an Air Raid Precautions (A.R.P.) warden, which meant that when the air raid warning sirens sounded, he, and a neighbour from No. 3, had to patrol the street to ensure that no light was showing from the house windows, and that no unauthorised persons were on the street. During their patrol, they met up with wardens from other stairs and, no doubt, compared notes. On the nights when Clydebank was being heavily bombed, people in Morningside claimed that they heard the German aircraft passing overhead en route to the west.

Morningside, however, had its own 'Dad's Army'. The Fairmilehead Home Guard Company operated from the summer of 1940 from its post in Buckstone Gardens until it was 'stood down' in the autumn of 1944. The comradeship which Home Guard members had enjoyed during the war was preserved by the formation of a club, which met, for some time, in the original Buckstone Gardens post before moving temporarily to the Liberal Party Rooms at No. 79 Morningside Road. Anxious, however, to return to the scene of their Home Guard days at Fairmilehead, members were delighted when premises were acquired in the former stables of Comiston House, the house by then being occupied as the Pentland Hills Hotel. The stables were trans-

Tin mugs and plates were the order of the day at dinner time. The 55th Boys' Brigade Company at camp at Skateraw in 1936. *Courtesy of W. R. Smith*

A typical camp layout of the 55th Boys' Brigade Company at Colwyn Bay in 1959. *Photograph by W. R. Smith*

Bill Whalley (right) as a student outside what was then Edinburgh University Men's Union in Park Place after he had won the University Athletic Club's Arthur Seat race in the early 1930s. *Courtesy of Michael Whalley*

Rev. Bill Whalley presiding at Communion at Newton
on Ayr Parish Church in 1972. *Courtesy of Mrs Eleanor Gibson*

The 55th Boys' Brigade Company led by the pipe band passing St Matthew's Parish Church
c. 1933. This was the pipe band's first public engagement. I am in the front row nearest to the
pavement. *Courtesy of the author*

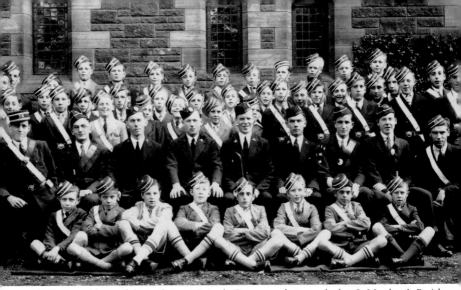

Officers and boys of the 55th Boys' Brigade Company photographed at St Matthew's Parish Church, *c.* 1935. In the second front row the staff sergeants and officers are, from left to right: Staff Sgt. Douglas Sutherland, Lt. Bob Downie, Lt. Archie Paul, Capt. Tom Taylor, Lt. Frank Somerfield, Staff Sgt. George Gordon and Staff Sgt. Bill Gannon. *Courtesy of W. R. Smith*

On the left, my brother William R. Smith, Captain of the 55th Boys' Brigade Company from 1950 to 1960, and on the right my father, Charles J. Smith who became Honorary Captain of the 55th. *Courtesy of W. R. Smith*

On the left, my father Charles J. Smith and on the right his brother, Bob, at the 55th Boys' Brigade Company camp at Linton, Kelso, *c.* 1941. *Courtesy of W. R. Smith*

Children of different ages, several of whom are wearing school caps, congregate for a street photograph in the backgreen of Maxwell Street, *c.* 1930. *Courtesy of W. R. Smith*

Looking east along the north side of Maxwell Street towards Braid Church (now Morningside Braid Parish Church). My mother and father came to a second-floor flat at No. 3 in 1924 where my brother and I spent most of our childhood. *Photograph by W. R. Smith*

My close boyhood friend, John Ramsay, volunteered for the Royal Air Force where he gained the rank of Sergeant Observer. He took part in many Lancaster bombing raids over Germany. Tragically, on 1 October 1942, at Syerston in Nottinghamshire, his Lancaster bomber, on take-off on a path-finding flight, developed a fault and crashed to the ground. *Courtesy of the author*

Morningside Family Laundry in Morningside Road was run by the Brotherston
family in the 1930s. The laundry was situated in the building which is now used
by the Angle Snooker Club. Beside the pavement, the shop used in connection
with the laundry, and the small flat above, were demolished many years ago for
the construction of a small supermarket which was later replaced by
Morningside Post Office. *Photograph by W. R. Smith*

A refreshment stop at the hut at Hillend Park in 1938. My Boys' Brigade pals,
from left to right are Frankie Spence, Ian Miller, George Ross and
Maurice Gunn. Neither Frankie nor Ian returned from the Second World War.
Courtesy of the author

Above: Early in the Second World War nurses and other staff were required to lend a hand to fill sandbags to protect the windows of the Astley Ainslie Hospital from damage by enemy action. The Astley Ainslie later became a military hospital. *Courtesy of Lothian Health*

Below: During the Second World War, Morningside had its own 'Dad's Army'. The Fairmilehead Home Guard Company operated from the summer of 1940 from its post in Buckstone Gardens. *Courtesy of the Fairmilehead Home Guard Snooker Club*

Catherine Violet Sands whom I married on 4 August 1945. Catherine was always happy to give me background support with my writing and lecturing and was greatly devoted to bringing up our family. *Courtesy of the author*

Catherine and I on our wedding day on 4 August 1945. We are seen here with our family and friends on the steps of the Chimes Private Hotel in Royal Terrace where the reception was held. *Courtesy of the author*

Jordan Lane looking west towards Morningside Road. This is about how I remember it as a child, completely devoid of motorised transport. *Courtesy of Malcolm Cant Publications*

My friend Wilfred Taylor, author and scholar, celebrated 'Scotsman's Log' writer for *The Scotsman* newspaper, lived at No. 14 Jordan Lane for over forty years. *Courtesy of Mrs D. Taylor*

In the 1920s Charles d'Orval Pilkington Jackson lived at No. 17 Jordan Lane where the author now resides. The photograph shows Pilkington Jackson in his studio at Polwarth Terrace at the planning stage of his most famous work, the Bruce statue at Bannockburn, which was unveiled on 24 June 1964.
Courtesy of The Royal Scottish Academy

Left – The five cousins at No. 17a Jordan Lane in 1962. My brother Bill's children are Pamela (third from the left) and Brenda (fourth from the left). Our children are Barbara (first from the left), Charles (second from the left) and Pauline on the extreme right.
Photograph by W. R. Smith

On holiday at Rothesay in 1970. From left to right: me, my wife Catherine, my father Charles J. Smith, my sister-in-law Sylvia, and my brother Bill. *Courtesy of the author*

Catherine and I and our two elder children in the back garden of No. 20 Jordan Lane in 1950. Barbara is on the left and Pauline on the right. *Courtesy of the author*

A crowded pier at Rothesay, probably during the Glasgow Fair, in the heyday of this popular Clydeside resort in the 1930s. *Courtesy of* The Herald and Evening Times

The Villa Cagnola, Varese, in northern Italy where I attended the churches' International Ecumenical Conference on laity responsibility, in 1965. *Courtesy of the author*

Members of the Standing Consultative Council on Youth Service in Scotland photographed on 1 November 1960. From left to right: Dr Reith; Charles J. Smith; Miss Mackenzie-Whyte; Mr Shirley; Dr Selby Wright; Dr Storrie; Mr Noble; Lord Kilbrandon; J. J. Farrell; Miss Hamilton; Dr Inglis; Mr Craig; Mr Duncan; Mr Brown; Mr Gray. *Courtesy of* The Herald and Evening Times

Sally McCabe, youth worker, with a group of children from the Hyve on an outing to the Zoo in the 1960s. *Courtesy of Mrs Sally Campbell (née McCabe)*

H. R. H. The Duke of Edinburgh arriving in Shandwick Place in May 1966 to attend a dinner at Norway House. I had the honour of receiving the Duke and introducing members of the Kilbrandon Council and other Edinburgh guests to him. *Courtesy of* Express Newspapers

H. R. H. The Duke of Edinburgh chatting informally to Lady Mar and the author before dinner at Norway House. *Courtesy of* Express Newspapers

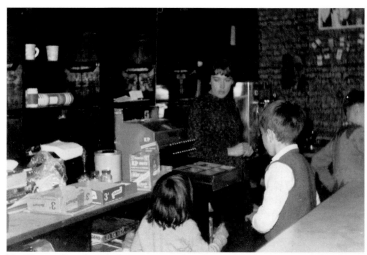

The Hyve café at the Youth Centre opened in the converted Hyvot's Bank farmhouse in 1964 was well attended. *Courtesy of Mrs Sally Campbell (née McCabe)*

Pentland Community Centre in Oxgangs Brae at the present day.
Courtesy of the author

formed into comfortable club rooms which are, nowadays, used by the Fairmilehead Home Guard Snooker Club.

In case it should be thought that the Second World War affected only the men of Morningside, it must be recorded that, as in other parts of the country, women over the age of eighteen were also required to register. They either worked in dangerous munitions factories or joined the women's services, such as the Women's Royal Navy Service (W.R.N.S.), the Auxiliary Territorial Service (A.T.S.), the Woman's Auxiliary Air Force (W.A.A.F.), or the Women's Land Army, many of them serving in important war zones.

Many men (and probably a number of women) from Morningside never returned from the war, including several comrades of my Boys' Brigade days. While there is a war memorial in Morningside Cemetery to those who fell in the First World War, there is no corresponding memorial for the Second World War. Perhaps it would now be impossible to obtain all the names. Fortunately, there are memorial tablets in many of Morningside's churches, but perhaps the time has now come for the various local organisations to consider erecting a war memorial to all those who fell in the Second World War.

FIVE

Home Life at Jordan Lane

WHILE THE Second World War had a traumatic effect the world over, it did not completely curtail the development of one's personal life. On 4 August 1945 I married Catherine Sands, a junior library assistant with Edinburgh City Libraries. We were on our honeymoon in the west of Scotland when the war came to an end. This was signalled by many ships on the Clyde sounding their sirens and spraying water in the air. We shared in the nation-wide relief that the war was over, but were sad for the many whose loved ones would never return. We could look forward, however, to the gradual ending of the many austerities which had been endured for six years.

Our first home was two furnished rooms, rented at No. 61 York Place. During our stay, we witnessed, at alarmingly close quarters beneath our windows, the serious fire which destroyed the Theatre Royal adjacent to St Mary's Roman Catholic Cathedral in Broughton Street. At the height of the blaze we were temporarily evacuated from our house for safety. It was just as well that our flat was furnished, since, during the war years, it was possible to buy only 'Utility' furniture of simple design and quality. We had time to wait until the situation improved, although we did, in fact, purchase and keep in store basic items such as a dining-room table, chairs and a wardrobe.

In 1947, we moved to one quite small room kindly provided by my father and mother in my old home at Maxwell Street. From there we bought a small flat at No. 22 Jordan Lane, where we were living when our two daughters, Barbara and Pauline, were born. It was not unusual for newly-married couples to begin in very modest accommodation. This was certainly very unlike the present day when many young couples, often with both parties in employment, obtain a mortgage and buy a reasonably-sized house before, if not soon after, their marriage.

Finally in 1954 we bought No. 17 Jordan Lane, jointly with my brother Bill and his wife Sylvia, and later subdivided the house for the respective families. The house had previously belonged to the Campbell family who ran several shops in Morningside. Jordan Lane seems to be known to many people in other parts of the city as a desirable place in which to live. I had known it well in my boyhood when we would cross the main road from Maxwell Street and explore the lane with its row of cottages on the south side, obviously dating back to when Morningside was a village. For us, there was a fascination about them, as if they were from another world. Half-way along the lane, also on the south side, there was, and still is, a large garage which we were told had once been a dairy with cows always kept indoors. Braid Hill Cottage was at the far end of the street, but where did the name come from? After all, the Braid Hills were some distance away. There was also the belief that there had once been a large farm between the end of Jordan Lane and Nile Grove, known as Egypt Farm. Here there had once been gypsies, some people said. Was this the derivation of the name 'Egypt'? All these intriguing stories meant that, for us, the lane never lost its fascination. These early memories were all still in my mind when we first heard of the sale of No. 17, which seemed to be the gateway to much which was still to be explored. It was a great day when, jointly with my brother and his wife, we acquired the house.

The house had a very large garden, and our part had a verandah, and several tall trees, including fir, cherry, apple and crab apple. There was also enough ground to grow vegetables. The lawn was welcomed by Barbara to practise the high jump in which she did well in the Edinburgh Inter-Scholastic Sports. Pauline was keener on tennis, not a few of her practice shots threatening our ground floor windows, and one, indeed, shattering the glass and ending up in our lounge. Charles, born after we had moved to No. 17B, first cultivated his football skills here, and for some time operated a bicycle repair and spare parts depot in an old shed. The large garden, with its trees and many hiding places, lent itself to imaginative young adventures, especially in what we called the secret passage at the foot of the garden, which, at one time, had given access from our, and neighbouring properties, to what were then fields leading to the Braid Hills, long before Nile Grove was built. Living adjacent to my brother and his family gave years of great happiness, especially for our children, who, like the adults, were always toing and froing. For many years we maintained our Easter tradition of rolling dyed, hard-boiled eggs, and exchanging chocolate eggs between our extended families. Happily, over a long period, my father and mother found great pleasure in the garden, frequently enjoying afternoon tea in the warm south-facing aspect. My mother was an enthusiastic jam-maker who transformed our crab apples, gooseberries and strawberries into tasty produce in her Maxwell Street kitchen. My father, even well into his eighties, was an invaluable gardener, even if he could not always distinguish between weeds and cultivated plants! In the autumn, his great delight was a roaring bonfire at the foot of the garden, with the flames kept going after dark, until he was finally summoned indoors.

We became quite interested in knowing who had lived previously in our house and discovered that it had been owned by Charles d'O. Pilkington Jackson, the noted sculptor, whose work included the Bruce Statue at Bannockburn and various sculptures at the Scottish National War Memorial at Edinburgh Castle. I was also privileged to have as a neighbour and friend, Wilfred Taylor (author of *Scot Easy* and *Scot Free*), the celebrated 'Scotsman's Log' writer who lived at No. 14. In his works he describes his part of Jordan Lane and his young family, in addition to quite famous previous residents in his house, including the eccentric landscape painter, Sam Bough, R.S.A., habitué of the nearby Canny Man's pub.

The two ladies who lived at No. 20 (then known as Braid Hill Cottage) were artists who had their kiln in the city where they produced pottery which was then handpainted by one of them. While we were still living at No. 22, they kindly gave me the use of a small plot of land in their garden in which to grow vegetables. The Jordan Burn flowed openly, and pleasantly, at the foot of this garden, and there was an old handle-operated draw pump. At the foot of my brother's garden, adjacent to ours, there was a stone-built washhouse with a boiler, believed to have been used for washing clothes. It is possible that, at one time, the water for washing was drawn up from the Jordan Burn below. There was a similar arrangement in the garden of No. 16 Jordan Lane. To complete the lane's notable residents, George Meikle Kemp, architect of the Scott Monument in Princes Street, lived in, and had a public funeral from, No. 5, still known as Ainslie Cottage.

While my family did not become closely involved with me in writing my earlier books, they readily accepted a father who so often seemed to be at his desk or ensconced in libraries – although he still managed to keep a large garden in reasonable order and reap a modest harvest. I realise now that they supported me and contributed perhaps much more than my previous book acknowledgments have expressed. Alan Sillitoe wrote *The Loneliness of the Long Distance Runner*, whilst others have written of the loneliness of the writer. This, in common with so many others, I have known.

There were, of course, many occasions when I had to abandon any attempt at writing for matters which were considered, at the time, to be much more important. When the legendary Beatles paid a visit to Edinburgh in April 1964, my daughters and a friend were anxious to obtain tickets for the event which was to be held in what was then known as the Regal Cinema (now the ABC) in Lothian Road. An announcement was made that tickets would be on sale at the box office from 7.00 a.m. on the morning of the concert. At about 10.00p.m. on the previous evening I joined the queue with a deck chair in one hand and a fish supper in the other. It was a long wearisome night but fortunately the box office opened an hour early and the queue began to move slowly, and in a very orderly manner, towards the cinema. With my precious three tickets in hand, and my wallet considerably lighter, I made my way home on foot. Alas, when I got to Jordan Lane I discovered that I had come away without my keys and the whole household was still asleep! I managed to climb onto the roof and get in by an attic window without arousing too much suspicion from the neighbours. Later, I gathered from my daughters that the concert had been well worth all the trouble. Perhaps the only disappointment for them was in not catching a glimpse of the 'Fab Four' as they left the venue. Apparently the shadows seen at the dressing-room windows were a decoy and the management had already arranged for the group to leave by another door. I was much more fortunate when I had the pleasure of meeting the Kinks personally when they arrived in a white Rolls Royce at a club in the High Street run by my friend Laurence Demarco.

My family also still often recall vividly, and with pleasure, the many happy holidays we enjoyed, frequently at Rothesay. Much of the pleasure and excitement was in getting there. For us, taxis were reserved for special occasions such as weddings or emergencies. But going to Rothesay was special, so, loaded with luggage, we took a taxi to Waverley Station and then the train to Glasgow Queen Street. If we went by Craigendoran, the journey was easy with a simple change of platform at Queen Street Station. However, if we went by Wemyss Bay it was necessary to cross Glasgow to Central Station. The station was thronged with would-be travellers some of whom watched intently for a board to be placed at an office window to indicate the platform number for the Wemyss Bay train. Usually it was number 13. There was a mad scramble up to the departure point, with everyone competing to get seats. Usually it was a single-compartment type of train without a connecting corridor. From the window we could see the great cranes above the famous, bustling Clyde shipyards until we were skirting Gourock and Greenock. Wemyss Bay was a beautifully kept station with floral baskets adorning the long enclosed passage down to the boat. Then it was anchors aweigh and with the thick ropes cast off we headed for Innellan. As we passed Toward Point, with its important lighthouse, we could see the great Arran peaks, known as the Sleeping Warrior, rising much higher than Canada Hill on Bute – so named when Rothesay people congregated there to watch the large ships taking emigrants across the Atlantic to Canada.

Soon we landed at Rothesay's crowded pier where we took the bus, or if funds rose to it a short taxi ride, to our holiday abode. There were various categories of accommodation. Sometimes it would be 'Room and Kitchen, Own Key' per the *Daily Record* advertisement, nowadays referred to as self-catering. Another grade of accommodation was known as 'Attendance' in which the landlady, living in another part of the house, cooked and served the food which guests themselves had bought.

Rothesay also had innumerable 'Board Residences', one of which we vividly and lovingly recall, because of its eccentricity. This was a fine villa which had seen better days but was still in business. When the proprietrix, a dear old lady of personality and not a little culture and charm, showed Pauline to her ground-floor room, she suggested that Pauline should ensure that the windows were always kept closed. Apparently there were rats in the back garden and it was best to keep them out. Pauline's face, as they say, was a study. The large painting of the Highland cattle above her bed, and the squeaking floor boards throughout the house, completed the scene. It was a house where time had stood still: even the black-out boards, used during the Second World War to cover the large sky-lights, were still in place. Just in case!

In earlier days we would walk past the steep steps leading from the promenade up to Rothesay's grandest residence, the Glenburn Hydropathic, whose residents we would see gazing down from the balcony. How wonderful it would be to stay in such an expensive and exclusive place. As the years passed, the time came when, almost unbelievably, we were being driven up to the impressive entrance and were checking in at reception. Hard work and a little of my book royalties had perhaps helped!

We have the happiest memories of Bute in the days when Rothesay was extremely popular as a holiday resort. Many fine steamers queued up to call at the pier each morning at 10.00 a.m., some of them listing over as the many passengers came to the side of the boat, either to go ashore or simply watch the scene on the pier, before sailing on to the Kyles of Bute, Arran, Largs, the Holy Loch, Campbeltown and Tarbert, or Ardrishaig and Inveraray on Loch Fyne.

Of all the Clyde steamers which sailed from the Broomielaw at Glasgow to Rothesay (such as *Waverley*, the *Duchess of Hamilton* or the *Queen Mary II*) perhaps the most interesting was MacBrayne's *Loch Fyne*. This sailed daily through the Kyles of Bute to Inveraray. It had a kind of Highland air about it as the crew wore Glengarry bonnets and sometimes the aroma of kippers wafted from the galley. This was the Royal Mail ship which took letters and parcels to many ports of call, from which deliveries were made by post bus to remote villages in Argyll and Kintyre. Often there were cattle on board and all kinds of commodities addressed to all sorts of places. On its daily return to Rothesay, boxes of herring would be off-loaded, heading for Rothesay's many kippering premises and fish shops, the smell frequently permeating every corner of the surrounding streets.

Frequently we went by bus, or on foot, to enjoy picnics in many of Bute's fine, sandy bays, looking out to Arran or the Cumbraes. There was the usual search for a burn to get water for our kettle which was boiled on a fire between large stones, using driftwood found on the beach. We erected our tent just in case rain – not unknown on the Clyde – drove us into shelter.

Rothesay, in these early days, was a bustling, lively place before cheap package holidays to Spain and other far-off climes were available. Montague Street, the 'back street', had attractive shops of all kinds, several of which sold model boats with sails or even an engine. Unfortunately, holiday pocket money was not usually up to it. The many excellent butchers, purveying Bute's fine home-produced meat, had window posters offering 'links', not the golfing kind, but sausages in Glasgow parlance. The Kiddies Corner, a small sandy shore, was crowded with ice-cream kiosks doing a roaring trade. Likewise the promenade was thronged with people, attracted to everything from roundabouts to bingo. In the evening, under the coloured fairy lights which stretched around the bay, there was a

queue for the famous Rothesay Entertainers, where several
notable Scottish comedians and singers first appeared. For
many years, the Rothesay Illuminations attracted boatloads
of sightseers from Dunoon and Largs. The electric lights
were augmented by what were known as Padella lights
which were placed along the promenade and also on the
window sills of countless boarding houses along the front.
Padella lights were like stubby candles which sat in a small
metal saucer with a raised rim.

If the Rothesay scene has been described in some detail, it
is to record an era long since past. Nowadays, Rothesay is
visited only by a fraction of the people who used to go there.
The many boarding houses, some of which were originally
impressive retirement houses of Glasgow merchants and
professional people, now have either closed or are restricted
to a short season. Change, however, is not always such a
bad thing. Although Rothesay itself is sadly no longer the
bustling resort it once was, a lot of effort is currently being
put into marketing the whole of Bute which offers horse
riding, walking, boating, fishing, music festivals and a
whole host of other interests.

Much of the interest, adventure and excitement of our
journeys to Rothesay in the past was linked to the time it
took to get there by train and boat. Nowadays, going by car
from Edinburgh, via the car ferry, is a very much quicker
journey. If time is less important, Rothesay can be reached
by a most pleasant car journey from Edinburgh to Loch
Lomond, and on to Arrochar, through Glen Croe, and by
Loch Fyne and Loch Riddon to the briefest ferry crossing at
Colintraive to Bute. Because of this mode of travel, many
holiday-makers do not stay on the island for more than a
few days. So much can be covered and seen by car.

As a result of my interest and involvement in the study of
social problems and the Christian approach to these, I was

invited to attend an international ecumenical conference on these subjects at Varese, near Milan in 1965. My family accompanied me by train which was then the cheapest means of travel. The conference was interesting and many world-wide contacts were made. The actual location was the Villa Cagnola in Gazzada. The vast and priceless collection of art work of all kinds, period furniture and unique treasures from its days as a private house were still in situ. It was a most elegant house with a fascinating atmosphere.

We long retained memories of this first venture abroad, even including the very early morning arrival by sleeper from Edinburgh to King's Cross Station in London where we spent a few days sightseeing. On arrival at Calais, after a stormy crossing on the Channel ferry, we missed the Paris train and had to complete the journey late at night, via Lille. We telephoned our Paris hotel to advise them of the delay and eventually arrived at the Hôtel de la Bourdonnais near the Eiffel Tower, in the early hours of the morning. We were received by an understandably rather displeased night porter who showed us to our rooms. Disturbing sleeping residents by treading on loose and squeaky floor boards was hardly calculated to improve the Auld Alliance.

After a day or two sightseeing we set out for the Gare de Lyon. Unfortunately, as we were carrying eleven suitcases and other bags (much of it because Pauline had enough clothes and make-up equipment to satisfy a film star) we required two taxis. Due to some confusion, Pauline and I found ourselves in the leading taxi, proceeding at great speed, followed by my wife, Barbara and Charles who were instructing their driver to try to catch up with us. The pursuing driver must have thought that Pauline and I were eloping and making our escape!

En route from Paris to Milan, we spent a day or two at Sion in the Rhône valley, visiting Montreux and a most picturesque little village above Lake Geneva, Les Avants, where I had once attended another conference. This was the location of several chalet schools and a notable skiing resort. From my visit to Switzerland so many years ago, and flying over it several times in recent years, I have never ceased to be overwhelmed by the limitless grandeur of the Alps. From Sion, we took an express train via Milan to Varese where we spent several days before continuing, by train, to Rome and the wonders of the Eternal City. Our return journey was by Würzburg and Ostend.

Travelling by train, even missing the correct one, and spending time in various European stations, provides the ideal opportunity to hear and attempt to be understood in other languages. Experiencing the atmosphere of the streets, of the shops, and residing with the local people, rather than in package tour hotels, provides an invaluable, almost indefinable educational and human experience, which as a family we have never lost. Such an experience occurred in Munich station after leaving Würzburg. Around midnight, when we were waiting for a night train, an old peasant man from Sicily, who was making his way through Germany, offered us some Chianti direct from the mouth of his large bottle, and a share of his bread and cheese.

As a result of being favourably impressed by our visit to Italy, Barbara and Pauline both decided to include Italian in their Edinburgh University Arts degrees. Later, Pauline attended several courses at Siena, Perugia and Urbino, and Barbara spent some time as a student engaged in an archaeological dig on the impressive medieval walls of Lucca, near Pisa, in Tuscany. She eventually settled in Lucca where we have enjoyed many family holidays with relatives and friends.

SIX

Youth and Community

IN THE late 1940s, several Sections, as they were called, of the Young Christian Workers' Youth Movement were established in Edinburgh and later in various parts of Scotland. In Edinburgh, one of these Sections was centred on Acheson House, close to Huntly House in the Canongate. The initiator was the late Rev. John Summers, a young Church of Scotland minister. Expressing his interest in, and lending support to this new approach to youth work, was the distinguished, and perhaps somewhat radical, Dr George MacLeod of Govan Parish Church and Iona (later Lord MacLeod of Fuinary) who pioneered the restoration of the ancient abbey and founded the Iona Community.

The unique feature of the Young Christian Workers' Movement was the living out of Christianity in everyday working life. The members were also known as Jocists, taken from the initials of the organisation Jeunesse ouvrière chrétienne internationale, founded by Canon Joseph Cardijn, a Roman Catholic priest in Brussels. A Section, either all boys or all girls, consisted of eight to ten members between the ages of fourteen and twenty, who met to study the Gospels in relation to everyday working life situations through a system of Social and Gospel Inquiries. In relation to the Social Inquiry, for example, the approach was one of SEE – JUDGE – ACT. The Section members considered the *facts* of a situation first (SEE). How many young people are employed in your work place? What are the age groups? What kind of work do they do? Do they have a proper training and apprenticeship system? Is it effective? Are they

paid a fair wage and given time off for study? Are they
members of their appropriate trade union and does it look
after their interests? Are accidents likely to occur? What
safety measures are in place? What is the moral atmosphere
of the work place? Is there equal respect for male and female
workers? Is bad language used and tolerated? The answers
could be quite revealing. Next, JUDGE. What do we think of
these situations in the light of the Gospels and Christian
teaching? Finally, ACT. If they are at variance with one
another, how can the situations be changed by the Section
members involved in their work place?

The Gospel Inquiry entailed a systematic, but not too
academic, study of one of the Gospels, recounting what
Christ said and did in particular situations. The question
then was how the Section members could apply the Gospel
teaching to their own work place or environment. As a
result of the facts brought to light (and it was part of the
formation and development of the young members to look
out for these facts) a question might have to be raised with
various people, including trade union representatives,
Safety at Work Inspectors, the press, and employers. The
facts had to be ascertained, a judgment made on these facts,
and the appropriate action taken.

The Section members could bring their non-member
friends (Christian or non-Christian) to regular open meetings for an evening of friendship and entertainment. The
Sections were linked by councils at local, national and
international levels. There were also Y.C.W. songs, which
reinforced a spirit of comradeship of a movement on the
march towards the best interests of young workers. The
main principle of the movement, inspired by Christian
ideals, was 'By young workers, for young workers'. The
aim was not to protect young people from an unsuitable
environment but rather to change it by their own action.

This movement attracted considerable attention amongst educationalists and Scottish government departments and agencies concerned with the apparently ever-present 'youth problem'. Having become leader of the Edinburgh Sections, I was invited to address important conferences in various parts of Scotland. Then in 1959 I was invited by the Rt. Hon. John McLay, then Secretary of State for Scotland, to become a member of the newly formed Scottish government body, the Standing Consultative Council on Youth and Community Service in Scotland or the Kilbrandon Council, which took its name from its chairman, the distinguished Scottish judge, Lord Kilbrandon. I was readily granted time off by my university head of department to attend the council's regular daytime meetings in St Andrew's House.

The Kilbrandon Council had been set up in Scotland soon after the Albemarle Council (named after Lady Albemarle) was established by the government for England and Wales. The creation of the latter had been accompanied by much media coverage of 'the youth problem'. The Albemarle Report praised the work being done for young people by the many long-established statutory bodies such as the Association of Boys and Girls Clubs, The Boys' Brigade, and the Boy Scout and Girl Guide Movements, which had trained leadership (much of it voluntary) and attractive premises and programmes. Nevertheless, it was observed that, in fact, very many young people were not attracted to the national youth organisations. It was also felt that there was a need for a more systematically-trained type of professional youth and community worker, in touch with young people's interests and needs in the 1960s.

The aim of the Kilbrandon Council, therefore, was to consider the status quo, to identify gaps in provision for young people, and to seek to improve the youth service generally by approaching the task with the expertise of the wide variety of the council's membership. The council was made up of representatives from the major youth organisations in Scotland, many of them highly experienced people; and educationalists, for example, the Principal of Moray House College of Education, and members of the Scottish Education Department.

One of the earliest steps was to establish a diploma course in youth and community work at Moray House. Qualified tutors were appointed and eventually a new department was established. The pioneer in this new undertaking by Moray House was Mr Brian Ashley. One of the aims of training an increased number of professionally qualified youth leaders and community workers was to encourage the national youth organisations and local authorities, which owned and ran youth centres and community centres, to employ the new qualified graduates from Moray House. At the same time, the Kilbrandon Council undertook to ensure that such graduates would be paid at nationally-negotiated salary scales. In other Scottish cities, the Moray House scheme was introduced in colleges of education, resulting in a considerable influx of qualified workers to the Scottish youth and community schemes. At the same time, grants were made available from the Scottish Education Department for youth organisations and local authorities to erect new purpose-built premises, often at considerable cost, with well-designed, modern facilities, and trained, salaried staff.

One interesting experience as a member of the Kilbrandon Council was to go on visits to new premises in various parts of Scotland, notably in Glasgow and Dumfries. In 1964 I personally paid an individual visit to the, then, newly-established Nechell's Green Community Centre in Birmingham, reporting back on my impressions to the Kilbrandon Council.

Undoubtedly, after the new schemes were implemented, a considerable boost was given to youth and community work in Scotland. After we had been in office for some years, the council's name was changed from 'Youth and Community Service' to simply 'Community Service' on the premise that since young people were part of the community, the title community service embraced all ages. Within the centres, of course, there were separate facilities for different age groups, each with their own leaders.

During our after-Council informal meetings, Lady Mar and I reached the view that while much effective work was being done in various areas, and by various agencies, there was often a tendency for the participants to be dealing with the same situations in isolation. We, therefore, thought that it might be worthwhile to invite people from different backgrounds and approaches to meet from time to time for a 'Dutch lunch'. These 'lunches', at which people paid for their own meal, were actually held in the evening, and became very popular. The venue was Norway House, an attractive West End restaurant in Shandwick Place, run by its Norwegian owner, Helge Weibye. Around thirty or more people attended, including youth workers, community workers, social workers, educationalists (including influential Scottish Education Department specialists), journalists, television presenters, certain police officers who were interested in our sphere of study, and clergymen of various denominations. Altogether, it was a fair cross-section of people, all of whom were interested in, and concerned with, the provision of leisure facilities in Edinburgh's new, or not so new, housing areas. After a modest meal, during which there was a great deal of interesting and informed conversation, the speaker would then describe his or her particular work in the field. In the following open discussion, often lively and frank, contributors would comment on the issues from their own special angle and experience. There were no formal conclusions, but frequently points were brought to light that were not known, or had not been thought about, by everyone present. By no means the least valuable feature of our 'Dutch lunch' evenings was the opportunity which people had to meet one another, often for the first time: useful contacts were made; diaries were brought out; and telephone numbers and the titles of publications were noted. I remember, particularly, that on one occasion, Father Borelli, a young priest who worked with homeless and vulnerable boys in Naples, was visiting Edinburgh. He gave a fascinating description of his work with the Naples *Scugnizzi*. On another occasion, Magnus Magnusson was our guest when he spoke on the place of the media in publicising youth problems and the role of youth organisations.

Word of our club spread and was the subject of conversation between the Duke of Edinburgh and Lady Mar when they met at Holyrood, as a result of which the Duke expressed the desire to attend one of our meetings when next he was in Edinburgh. Thus, one evening in May 1966, Shandwick Place was packed with onlookers to watch the Duke being received by Lady Mar and me at Norway House. Inside, forty guests waited expectantly for the arrival of His Royal Highness. I had the rather anxious task of ensuring that our royal guest met each of those present for a brief word, rather than being waylaid by any one person. The meal was given the special attention of Mr Weibye, the Norwegian restauranteur, who had brought over Norway's premier chef for the occasion.

At the coffee stage, as co-host with Lady Mar, I invited discussion from the guests. The Duke himself put some very relevant questions to those working in the field, which produced further lively discussion. This special evening was a great stimulus for our future gatherings, but they were eventually discontinued when it was thought that their purpose had been served.

While the Kilbrandon Council appeared to have followed, successfully, its remit to encourage and support the development of youth and community work, nevertheless, certain members of the council began to promote discussion on the problem of what were popularly termed 'the unclubbables'. This was not intended as a judgmental description of the many young people (thought to be two-thirds of those between the ages of fourteen and twenty) who were not attracted by the facilities offered by the more traditional youth organisations or clubs. It was felt that many of the 'unclubbables' were the very people who would benefit most from discovering useful and interesting ways of spending their leisure time. Of course, there were just no leisure facilities in many of Scotland's vast new housing areas. The bleakness and boredom in these housing estates was expressed graphically by a young boy who was being interviewed by a group of social researchers. When asked where he lived, he replied: 'In a graveyard with lights': still, unfortunately, a vivid picture of the environment of very many young people in Scotland.

Early in 1964, the Countess of Mar and Kellie, president of the Scottish Association of Youth Clubs, and a member of the Kilbrandon Council, and I began to discuss the challenge of the 'unclubbables'. Following a meeting of the council, we would go to a café or restaurant for afternoon tea. Lady Mar had a lively mind and brought enthusiasm to many subjects which were of concern to her. We talked about some new kind of approach, distinct from the traditional youth organisations and clubs. In fact, in Edinburgh and Glasgow, experimental work was already being done through the employment, by local authorities or youth club councils, of what were known as 'detached youth workers'. These workers, both men and women, had graduated from courses at Moray House and other colleges. They simply frequented cafés in housing schemes, or inner cities, and got to know young people who also used the cafés as a place to meet and talk. Conversations arose as to the needs of a district in terms of its leisure facilities etc. The aim was to enlist young people who might be cynical and pessimistic about their district – like the boy who said that he lived in 'a graveyard with lights'. The idea was that the detached worker would encourage or persuade young people to take the initiative in improving their local situation, and it met with moderate success.

The early 1960s was the era of The Beatles and other pop groups, most of which were able to attract a large following among the young people of the day. Lady Mar and I wondered if there was some way in which we could 'cash in' on the phenomenon of the pop world. Our vision – yes, it was that – was to acquire premises in an area of the inner city or in one of the new housing areas. We heard about suitable premises in Dalry Road, consisting of an unused part of a factory, but, unfortunately, the rent was prohibitive. We also visited a former billiards saloon in Craigmillar, in the days before snooker was such a popular sport, but again were not successful, which was a great pity as Craigmillar would have been a very challenging district. However, our hopes were again raised in 1964 when an advertisement appeared in the Edinburgh press for the sale of Hyvot's Bank farmhouse with stables and a large corrugated iron shed. Hyvots was situated in the large new housing area at Gilmerton which was estimated to have a youth population of around 7,000. In speculating on the possibility of opening a dance hall with café facilities, we were greatly encouraged by the interest shown, and the

practical advice given, by my close friend, Laurence Demarco, already well-established in the Edinburgh café
world.

One May morning, having first advised Lady Mar, who
lived in Alloa, Laurence and I headed with all speed to
Hyvot's Bank. His inherited Italian flair for creating attractive cafés was immediately apparent. He saw so many
possibilities: the stables could be converted into an attractive café area with tables in the former horse stalls; and a
very large room adjoining the farmhouse could be floored
over for dancing, with a raised platform at one end for the
entertainers. The many rooms in the spacious, adjacent
farmhouse could be used for various interest groups such
as a beauty parlour, a billiards room and a room for
photography. Laurence thought that the large corrugated
iron shed would be ideal for indoor football and, altogether,
the whole place seemed to be perfectly suited to our re-
quirements. The Hyve, as it came to be known, was staffed
by two female youth leaders, trained at Moray House,
taking on duties rather like the Red Coats at holiday camps.

We soon conveyed our enthusiasm to Lady Mar who
visited the site without delay. Her enthusiasm knew no
bounds – which made three of us! There was only one
problem and that, predictably, was the cost. I cannot now
recall what price had been placed on the premises by
Edinburgh Corporation, but whatever they were asking,
it was beyond our means. On the other hand, there was just
a possibility that it could be affordably rented. Lady Mar
and I arranged to meet the Lord Provost of the day, Sir
Herbert Brechin, who listened intently as Lady Mar presented our case with characteristic enthusiasm. Sir Herbert
expressed his immediate approval of the whole project and
announced that we could have the farmhouse, and all the
outbuildings, for a nominal rent.

There were, of course, several practicalities still to be addressed. The task of converting the stables and outbuildings fell upon the shoulders of Laurence Demarco and his team of builders and joiners. Although we received grant aid for the project, Laurence also invested a considerable sum from his own capital to run the café and pay the staff.

The Hyve opened to great acclaim in the autumn of 1964. Repeated press advertisements announced this 'New Place to Go'. The *Evening News and Dispatch* for 11 August 1964 described the Hyve under the headline 'A Club by a Babbling Brook', a reference to the Burdiehouse Burn which skirted the premises. Another article under the heading 'An Edinburgh Club with a difference' commented that although the premises had been extensively altered, 'the atmosphere has not been lost'. On the opening night, the two specially trained Moray House youth workers were lined up ready to act as café assistants, and an established pop group was tuned up to get the dancing going. When the doors opened, we were swamped by young people of a wide age range, mostly from the surrounding areas, but some from other parts of the city. By the time the youth workers, who resided in the farmhouse, crawled off to bed we knew we had a success.

The Hyve opened its doors night after night. Apart from their evening and late-night commitment to the project, the two youth workers organised outings to the Zoo and other places, which were greatly enjoyed by the older children during the school holidays. Early in 1965 it was calculated that, from a catchment area of about 7,000, approximately four hundred young people were attending the Hyve in the course of a week, each paying a membership fee of five shillings (25p) per year. However, as the summer approached, it was found that the numbers were dwindling and that funds were insufficient to meet the cost of repairing the damage which was being caused to the building by some of the young people. On one occasion the electric meter was vandalised, which was particularly dangerous. By May 1965 the problems were much worse. There was frequently an atmosphere of tension in various areas, created by a prevalence of noise and fighting among the people attending. After the premises were closed at the end of the evening, many young people hung around outside, showing obvious aggression. As the destruction of property increased, including damage to cars parked in nearby streets, the two youth workers felt that there was a crisis and that the situation had come to a head.

The various problems had been regularly reported to the management committee chaired by the Countess of Mar. It was decided that the two youth workers should call a meeting of all Hyve members who were interested in discussing the future. About forty members attended the meeting at which it was explained that, because of continuing problems and financial loss, the Hyve might have to close. Many of the members expressed mock regret and were quite cynical, whereas others were genuinely upset at the threat of closure. The meeting was informed that, provided the Hyve members ceased their destruction and disruption, various adult groups in the district were prepared to support the Hyve and pay for the use of the facilities. The interested groups included a nursery for children, meetings for older people, and bingo sessions. The meeting eventually broke up after being given a challenge to repair the damaged areas. Some members, willing to help, remained behind and were allocated tasks including plumbing and joinery. Some repair work began and a night watchman was appointed to guard the property, both of which created an air of optimism and shared responsibility.

Unfortunately, shortly afterwards, it was found that the

café and dance area had made substantial losses and was no longer commercially viable. The Hyve closed down in late 1965. In the inevitable post-mortem, it emerged that many young people in the district were reluctant to spend their leisure time at the Hyve, which was on their doorstep, for the simple reason that if they misbehaved, or became boisterous or unruly, perhaps requiring police action, the news of their behaviour was all round the district next day. Many thus preferred to spend their spare time, anonymously, in clubs in the centre of the city. Whether the opening of such a club in a similar district, today, might be useful is very doubtful, particularly in view of the use of drugs which were not so generally available in the 1960s.

The Hyve was an enterprising and imaginative experiment and lessons were learned. If there was such a concept as 'the youth problem', solutions, or partial solutions, would have to be sought in other ways.

In 1964 Edinburgh Corporation Education Department advertised for four community development officers to work in various parts of the city. On the strength of my membership of the Kilbrandon Council and involvement in the Hyve youth project, I was appointed to one of the posts. The city was divided into four areas, each with its own officer. The areas were: Willowbrae, Portobello, and Craigentinny; Gilmerton, Southfield, Southhouse and Liberton; Wardie, Muirhouse, Drylaw and Granton; and Colinton Mains, Firrhill, Oxgangs, Craiglockhart, Colinton and Juniper Green. I was allocated this last area. As the job entailed evening work only, I remained with the Bacteriology Department at the university.

In my area, Colinton Mains Residents' Association had been established for a long time with a base in the buildings previously used by Colinton Mains farm, but the corresponding association for Craiglockhart had only recently been formed. Colinton and Juniper Green had long-established residents' associations and required little help from me. Firrhill and Oxgangs were fairly recently-built housing areas, the former dominated by the three high-rise towers, Caerketton, Allermuir and Capelaw Court. Oxgangs was the newest part and had not yet been completed. The area had several churches, namely St John's Church of Scotland, Colinton Mains Parish Church, St Mark's Roman Catholic Church, and St Hilda's Scottish Episcopal Church. The schools were Firrhill Senior Secondary School, Oxgangs Primary School, St Mark's Roman Catholic School and Hunters Tryst School. In addition to the residents' associations, there were Parent-Teacher Associations, the Co-operative Women's Guild, evening continuing studies groups and church organisations, many of which had been established when the houses were first built. Of particular note was the initiative and dedication of the Rev. John Orr, of St John's Church of Scotland on Oxgangs Road North, whose pioneering work made his church a kind of community centre. Oxgangs Residents' Association was the last of these organisations to be formed in my area, mainly through the efforts of a group of local men who met regularly in the Good Companions Roadhouse in Oxgangs Bank, and who were concerned about local needs and problems.

It was in the Colinton Mains, Firrhill and Oxgangs districts that my main work lay, the object being 'to enable' this extensive area of the old and the new to develop further a sense of community, based on its origins and location. I had known the districts of Oxgangs and Colinton Mains since my childhood when my parents took Bill and me on Sunday afternoon walks from Morningside, through Braidburn Valley, to Oxgangs farmhouse and Colinton Mains. In these days, a popular country walk was by the little wooden footbridge over the burn at the south end of Braidburn

Valley, along the path leading to Oxgangs farmhouse and Colinton Mains, and up what is now Oxgangs Road North, past the Cockit Hat wood and Hunters Tryst, to Swanston. If we were still feeling energetic, we climbed Caerketton to complete our walk. Several years later, a group of us older 55th Boys' Brigade members took the same route on Sunday afternoons, again with the top of Caerketton as our target. I developed a great liking for the area, but Firrhill hardly existed as a separate district then.

I worked in my fairly large area three evenings per week. My first tasks were to find out what organisations already existed, how often they met, and whether or not they were in good heart. I was welcomed by the office-bearers of the various organisations, through the city community development officer, Alex Fraser, a man with considerable knowledge and enthusiasm for the task. My colleagues, working in other parts of the city, and I, met with Mr Fraser at regular intervals to discuss progress and to share ideas.

As the various organisations and groups in the district followed their own aims and programme, they tended, understandably, to operate in isolation from one another. It seemed to me that it could be beneficial in many ways if there were some way to bring them together in a joint body. Indeed, without being doctrinaire in approach, it seemed from experience in other parts of the city, and cities elsewhere, that a community association was the answer. This could have advantages in relationships with the local authority and other bodies. At that time, of course, it was not foreseen that community councils for defined areas would be created as part of local government legislation.

The question was what would encourage the many and varied organisations to meet from time to time to discuss matters of common interest? With the encouragement of Alex Fraser, all the local organisations in the district thought about staging an annual festival with contributions from local groups in much the same way as had been done, so successfully, at the annual Pilton Festival. The idea took off, not least through the efforts of the Rev. John Orr and his church's Women's Guild.

In April 1964 the first Pentland Festival was held, which lasted for three days. But why the name? As a token of unity, this title was found to be acceptable to all the local groups, whose members lived against the common back-cloth of the nearby Pentland Hills. Incidentally, while our festival committee was first to adopt this district name, it was later used as the name of the parliamentary constituency. Our festival programme logo was the Pentland ridge in silhouette.

The main events of the festival were held in Hunters Tryst Primary School which had an excellent auditorium with a stage and other facilities. The varied programme included one-act plays, children's ballet groups, local school performances, and excerpts from popular stage musical comedies by one of the ladies' groups. I remember, particularly, at one of the early festivals, a local pop group took the stage, their output greatly enhanced by amplifiers. When the group struck their first note, the younger members of the large audience rose to their feet en masse, screaming and shouting their appreciation. They moved towards the stage, carrying all other members of the audience before them. These included a front row of VIPs, including Lord Provost Herbert Brechin and the Lady Provost, Scottish Education Department officials and local clergy. I remember feeling embarrassed, as the appearance of the pop group had been my suggestion. Had it been unwise? When comparative normality returned and the VIPs gathered in a back room for refreshments after the show, I was most relieved, and not a little surprised, to find that they had all enjoyed the entertainment. The following day, the press highlighted the fact that Dr George Reith, the city's Director of Education, had described the festival as 'an exciting venture with an important significance for the future'.

The Pentland Festival became an important annual stimulus, focal point and unifying factor for the whole area. The festival committee became an important body. A great spirit of collaboration developed and many friendships were made between members. It was also a financial success, which enabled the committee to purchase its own stage equipment.

This happy state of affairs also allowed the people of Colinton Mains, Firrhill and Oxgangs to feel part of a wider community. One of the resolutions of the Kilbrandon Council empowered local authorities to provide purpose-built modern community centres in areas where these would be most beneficial. The leaders of each of the authorities were in no doubt that they deserved, and would benefit from, a new community centre. In the Pentland area, discussion originally focused on the provision of separate youth and community centres, perhaps requiring buildings of different design. Eventually, however, the idea of accommodating all age groups in one suitably-designed building was accepted, and later implemented.

At an early stage, public meetings were called in my area, with local town councillors in attendance. Plans for a new community centre were drawn up, and agreed, after details had been made available to the public. I have never been clear why it was decided to erect the building in its present position eastwards of the Good Companions. It has always seemed to me that it would have been better for the new community centre to have been built at the south-west boundary of Colinton Mains public park. It would then have been almost equally accessible to the residents of both

Colinton Mains and Oxgangs. While the community centre bears the name Pentland, which was acceptable to the three districts, Colinton Mains, Firrhill and Oxgangs, the name Oxgangs for the library seems inappropriate. And again, why was it not situated further north as I proposed for the community centre? Whatever the issues, both the community centre (now the Pentland Community Education Centre) and public library have proved invaluable assets to the area.

A number of other developments in my former community development area merit congratulations and appreciation for the efforts of their initiators. The Oxgangs Gala Day has now become a most enjoyable occasion, with participation from a wide area. The Oxgangs Local History Association, very closely associated with the local public library, and drawing members from a wider area than its name suggests, provides a most interesting programme of summer walkabouts and winter talks. This obvious sign of the area's maturity and sense of its own heritage is to be welcomed. Also, *The Pentland Review*, a most stimulating and professionally-produced local periodical, reflected the wide range of events in the area until 1999 when it ceased production. It is to be hoped that this is only temporary.

SEVEN

University Career

WHEN I was at Boroughmuir School in the early 1930s, I did not apply myself as fully as I might have done. Consequently, in 1934, when my father was again without employment and the family budget was tight, I decided, without any great merit on my part, to leave school and find a job, thus contributing a little to the family budget. At age fourteen I left school without any certificates. I immediately, however, applied for a vacancy which was advertised in the *Edinburgh Evening News* for a 'lab boy' in the Bacteriology Department of Edinburgh University Medical School. I had no references, but, on the advice of my father, I mentioned in my letter of application that at the 55th Boys' Brigade Company I had won the Edinburgh Battalion First Aid Shield and gained a basic knowledge of anatomy and physiology. In my interview with Professor T. J. Mackie, Head of the Bacteriology Department, I expressed my interest in medicine, as a result of which I was offered the post despite my poor school performance. A main condition of acceptance was that I would undertake further evening study at what was then Heriot Watt College in Chambers Street. It was made clear to me that I needed to reach a level in Mathematics, Physics and Chemistry approximately equal to the Ordinary National Certificate, which would enable me to enter the training course for a qualification from the Pathological and Bacteriological Laboratory Assistants' Association.

Five years after I began work, I qualified – and the Second World War broke out. I was in what was known as a reserved occupation, and was therefore exempt from military service. Some, who were permitted to volunteer, were drafted into the laboratories of the Royal Army Medical Corps, either home-based, or attached to combatant units at various battle fronts where penicillin was used for the first time under hostile fire.

As the war progressed, and sources of important basic laboratory reagents from the Far East were threatened, attempts were made to obtain these from within Britain. These were tested for their efficacy in the Edinburgh University Bacteriology Laboratory. An important example was agar, a form of seaweed from Japanese waters, vital in the production of culture medium for growing bacteria. Seaweed from Scottish coasts was tried out, initially by the Marine Biological Research Station at Millport and then in our laboratories, as a substitute for Japanese agar, and found to be effective.

At first, it was feared that all of Britain would be subject to systematic air raids. While this was so in London, and several other English cities, most of the significant bombing in Scotland was confined to Clydeside. Nevertheless, certain precautions had to be taken by the authorities as other cities were attacked to a lesser extent. In addition to the relatively small corrugated-iron Anderson air-raid shelters in people's back gardens and some public parks, sizeable concrete shelters were built in the back greens of many Edinburgh tenements. Consideration had to be given to possible infection hazards facing people who might have to spend most nights sleeping in such confined shelters. A decision was taken by the Edinburgh Public Health Department that experimental work should be carried out under the direction of Dr H. E. Seiler, then Senior Depute Medical Officer of Health. I was very much involved in this. Groups of soldiers from Redford Barracks and people from the Auxiliary Fire Service were chosen to spend successive nights in selected back green shelters. In the Roseburn Terrace shelters, I exposed glass

Petri dish culture plates at various points while the volunteers were asleep in beds quite close to each other. The plates were exposed for fixed periods of thirty minutes. They were eventually all closed and taken back in the early morning to the laboratory and incubated for forty-eight hours. After this period, the plates were examined to identify the various types of bacteria which had grown. Their significance was later assessed by the Department. Some years later, this air-raid shelter work was incorporated with important research into air-borne droplet infection undertaken by Dr (later Professor) J. P. Duguid of our department.

Thankfully, Edinburgh was never subjected to systematic air raids by German planes as they passed over the city en route for Clydebank. While many people retired to their private shelters when the air-raid sirens sounded, there was not much overnight occupancy of the larger communal shelters. Outbreaks of air-borne infections did not, therefore, materialise.

Base or Emergency Hospitals, such as Peel, Law Junction, Bangour and Killearn were established to receive casualties in the armed forces, transported back to Scotland from the front line, for example after D-Day. In Morningside, the Astley Ainslie Hospital became an important military hospital, staffed jointly by services and civilian medical and nursing personnel. It was our task in the Medical School Bacteriology Department to equip the laboratories in these hospitals and to delegate skilled academic and technical staff. In addition, the Scottish Command Laboratory was also located for some years in the department.

One of the most historic discoveries in medical science was that of penicillin by the Scottish microbiologist Sir Alexander Fleming. Although the discovery was made in 1928 his report did not appear until the following year. The discovery was made when Fleming was working in his

New University Buildings, Teviot Place, *c.* 1913, home of the Medical School of Edinburgh University. *Courtesy of Malcolm Cant Publications*

Edinburgh University staff football team in the Lothian Amateur League in 1937. I am the second player from the left in the back row. *Courtesy of the author*

Sir Alexander Fleming discovered penicillin in his laboratory at St Mary's Hospital, Paddington in 1928. *Photograph from* Sir Alexander Fleming: Man of Penicillin

A teaching laboratory in the Medical Microbiology Department of Edinburgh University Medical School in 1985. *Courtesy of the Department of Medical Microbiology, University of Edinburgh*

In the centre, *c.* 1939, is Professor T. J. Mackie head of the Bacteriology Department when I first joined the staff in 1934. He is flanked by senior colleagues who all became professors in other universities. From left to right are Dr Scott Thomson, Dr C. A. Green, Dr Colin Beattie, and Dr C. E. van Rooyen who became a world pioneer virologist. *Courtesy of the Department of Medical Microbiology, University of Edinburgh*

Mr A. B. Cheyne (my predecessor) with members of staff and other senior colleagues on the day of his retirement as Senior Chief Medical Laboratory Technologist in the Bacteriology Department, 1964. The front row, from left to right, shows: Dr M. A. Latif, Charles J. Smith, A. B. Cheyne, John Brennan and Dr R. B. Singh. *Courtesy of the Department of Medical Microbiology, University of Edinburgh*

Professor J. G. Collee makes the presentation in the presence of senior colleagues of the Medical School at my retirement from the Department of Medical Microbiology in 1982. *Courtesy of The Scotsman Publications Ltd*

Ian Bannen, who visited my home in Jordan Lane, was a frequent performer at the Edinburgh Festival. He is seen here on the extreme left as 'Hickey' in The Iceman Cometh at the Royal Lyceum Theatre in 1974. The other performers are, from left to right, Muriel Romanes, Oscar James, Paul Young, James Grant and Leonard Maguire. *Courtesy of The Scotsman Publications Ltd*

Madeleine Renaud and Jean-Louis Barrault in La Répétition at the Edinburgh International Festival in 1957. *From Edinburgh International Festival Souvenir Programme 1957*

The Festival's international status was greatly enhanced in the early days by the appearance of Juliette Greco, the French singer. *Photograph by Paul Shillabeer in 1961. Courtesy of Edinburgh International Festival*

Duncan Macrae as 'The Pardoner' in the Edinburgh Festival production of The Three Estates in 1948. *Courtesy of Scottish Theatre Archives, Glasgow University Library*

During my research into the origins of the name Egypt in Morningside I had the pleasure of meeting the self-styled king of the Scottish gypsies, Charles Douglas (right) at Larkhall in the early 1970s. *Courtesy of the author*

The Rt. Hon. Robin Cook M.P., Secretary of State for Foreign and Commonwealth Affairs. In 1977 when Mr Cook was Assistant Director of the Edinburgh Workers' Educational Association he invited me to contribute a course of lectures under the title 'Historic South Edinburgh'. *Courtesy of The Rt. Hon. Robin Cook M.P.*

Basil Skinner, former Assistant Keeper of the Scottish National Portrait Gallery, was Director of the Extra-Mural Department of Edinburgh University when he invited me to contribute a series of lectures on 'Historic South Edinburgh' in 1979. *Courtesy of Mrs Lydia Skinner*

John G. Gray, my friend and co-author of *A Walk on the Southside in the footsteps of Robert Burns*, photographed in 1982 when he was President of the Society of Solicitors in the Supreme Courts of Scotland. *Photograph by L. W. Nimmo Courtesy of Mrs Elizabeth Gray*

Charles Skilton, publisher, outside his home at Banwell Castle
in Somerset in 1986. *Courtesy of Paul Harris, publisher*

An appreciative audience at the launching of my book *Edinburgh's
Contribution to Medical Microbiology* at the Royal Society of Edinburgh
on 30 June 1994. *Photograph by W. R. Smith*

On 25 November 1995 I was awarded an honorary degree of Bachelor of Science by the University of Edinburgh. The photograph is taken outside the McEwan Hall with Pauline, Charles and Barbara. *Photograph by W. R. Smith*

The author addressing a group of hospital staff and their friends during a conducted tour of the historic grounds of the Astley Ainslie Hospital on 29 January 2000. *Photograph by W. R. Smith*

laboratory at St Mary's Hospital, Paddington, but for several reasons outwith his control Fleming was not able to develop his ideas further. This was done in Oxford by the Australian microbiologist Sir Howard Florey and his German colleague Ernst Chain. After the publication of their work in *The Lancet* in late 1941, Edinburgh's Professor (later Sir) James R. Learmonth of Systematic Surgery became greatly interested in the possible use of penicillin for the treatment of surgical infections. Professor Learmonth persuaded my chief, Professor T. J. Mackie, to produce a supply of penicillin, which was very scarce, for clinical trials in Edinburgh Royal Infirmary. I was privileged to be a member of the small team assigned to this important task. My colleagues were Dr (later Professor) J. P. Duguid, Dr S. W. Challinor, and Mrs Jean McNaughton.

In the early work of Florey and Chain, it had been difficult to obtain a sizeable yield of the antibiotic when its source, the mould *Penicillium notatum*, was cultivated in a fluid culture medium. The mould required oxygen for growth and therefore grew on the surface of the medium. My job was to prepare Czapek Dox mineral salts solution, in special flat bottles with a relatively large surface area to give a fair yield of the mould. By September 1943, we had produced a yellow powder containing one million units of penicillin which was sufficient for Professor Learmonth to treat a patient with staphylococcal septicaemia and brain abscess. Initially the treatment was very successful but sadly, the supply of penicillin was exhausted and the patient died.

Meantime, British microbiologists had gone to the United States where they eventually persuaded Pfizer to undertake large-scale production of the antibiotic as a result of which further clinical trials were possible – often with dramatic results. With the substantial commercial production in America and eventually Britain, our modest efforts ceased. Other important antibiotics were, of course, to follow in the wake of penicillin: indeed at the present day many life-threatening bacteria have become resistant to antibiotics. Much new research in the fight against infection is under way.

Wartime produced many interesting anecdotes in the annals of the Bacteriology Department. During the war, the army was stationed on Inchcolm in the Firth of Forth. There, a soldier discovered a rather mysterious large glass vial, about six inches in length and about four inches in diameter, containing a clear fluid. There was a lot of speculation in the department about what the fluid was and where it had come from. Was this some form of bacteriological or chemical warfare, involving a drop by German planes? The department was alerted and the vial brought to us with great care to avoid breakage. When it arrived in the laboratory there was a small team wearing white coats and rubber gloves, lined up at the bench, under the direction of Professor Mackie. I was at his side, with a large bowl of strong iodine solution ready to wipe the vial with cotton wool soaked in the antiseptic to prevent any atmospheric contamination. The vial was marked with a glass file, in order to allow it to be cracked open, and with large, heavy, sterilised forceps Professor Mackie struck the vial a sharp blow, away from himself and over a basin full of disinfectant. Unfortunately, a small drop of the mysterious fluid splashed up onto the Professor's wrist. Within seconds it began to create a burning sensation on his skin, as though it were a strong acid. Professor Mackie quickly washed his wrist under running water and applied a disinfectant swab. Meantime, the biochemist in our team did a quick test which suggested that the fluid was indeed concentrated acid. In fact, later tests confirmed that it was concentrated sulphuric acid. This seemed an unlikely chemical weapon. Someone suggested that it might even be a long-hidden relic of manufacture by the monks of the twelfth-century Abbey of Inchcolm. We never actually found out, but the Professor led us in an all-round laugh at our dramatic approach to a suspected secret weapon!

Staff in the Medical School had to take their turn on the rota for firewatching, which entailed remaining overnight in a small room on the top floor of the building. If the air raid warning siren sounded, we had to be on the alert in case an incendiary bomb was dropped by a plane onto the roof. If such an event occurred, we were under strict instructions to soak the bomb with a strong jet of water from a stirrup pump, until the arrival of the fire brigade.

In 1941, the Polish School of Medicine was established within the Medical School in Teviot Place, and the opening ceremony was performed by the President of Poland, W. Raczkiewicz. The Polish School was staffed by Polish professors and doctors in collaboration with Edinburgh University medical staff. The Polish teaching staff and students had escaped from their own country during the German invasion and occupation. I arranged laboratory accommodation for a small number of Polish personnel, and assisted them in their work in our department. An account of the establishment of the Polish Medical School and its background can be seen on a wall plaque just inside the main gate of the Medical School in Teviot Place. In 1992 *In the Dark Days of 1941* was published to commemorate fifty years of the Polish School in Edinburgh.

After the war, I was given several tasks which were of particular interest to me. The first of these was the regular testing of commercially manufactured catgut, or surgical sutures, to ensure that these were sterile. The makers were bound by law to submit to our department random samples representing a percentage of the total batch produced. Very careful testing was carried out over a period of fourteen days, after which we reported our findings. If the all-clear was given, the sutures could then be supplied to general medical practitioners or to hospitals for surgical use. I do not recall any batch ever being found to be significantly contaminated. We carried out similar testing on ampoules of BCG vaccine (bacille Calmette-Guérin) in the early days of its use for tuberculosis vaccination.

Another of my tasks was to examine rats, which had been gassed and taken from ships arriving at Leith Docks from abroad, to ensure that the vermin were not carrying bubonic or pneumonic plague. For many years I was also responsible for the examination of fish, principally salmon, from rivers in Scotland and certain parts of England. To the great concern of local bailiffs and later the Scottish Department of Agriculture and Fisheries, large numbers of fish had been found dying, or dead, in rivers. My chief, Professor T. J. Mackie, was the official fish examiner for Scotland.

One of my chiefs, Professor Robert Cruickshank, a close colleague of Sir Alexander Fleming, was an expert consultant with the World Health Organization in Geneva. This work took him to many parts of the world, including Pakistan and India, to advise on health problems, especially infectious diseases. During his trips, if he met doctors involved in bacteriology who wished to pursue postgraduate studies, he would invite them to our department in Edinburgh. A laboratory was set aside and equipped for these doctors which, at one time, was sufficiently large to earn the description of 'The Great Eastern Laboratory'. For two years I worked with Dr S. K. Biswas, of Calcutta, who was awarded a Ph.D. degree for his important work in the laboratory diagnosis of syphilis.

Perhaps one of the most interesting and certainly most challenging projects in which I was ever involved arose a year or so before my retirement in 1982. This was in assisting the distinguished virologist, Professor Barrie Patrick Marmion, to design a Category A laboratory for use in the emergency diagnosis of highly dangerous pathogens such as those responsible for rabies and Lassa fever, should such cases ever occur in Edinburgh or the surrounding area. The highly skilled virologists engaged in handling these organisms had to be given a high degree of protection during the procedures in the laboratory. Situated in the Medical School tower high above the Middle Meadow Walk and Teviot Place, the laboratory was divided into clean and infected areas. Personnel first entered the clean area, in which they undressed completely and put on a special safety gown and mask. The clean area led into a shower chamber, from where, now gowned and masked, the person passed into the infected area, closing a sliding door behind him. Having done this, he could not return to the clean area without first discarding his mask and gown in the infected area, and then taking a shower. Special 'absolute' air filters made it certain that no airborne infection could escape externally, and a complex ventilation system ensured that the airflow continuously passed from the clean area into the infected area and never in the reverse direction. The potentially infected water from the shower was first heated in a sterilising tank before being discharged into the ordinary drain. A special visit was made by fire fighters in a number of fire engines, including one with a long ladder capable of reaching the tower laboratory windows from Teviot Place. They rehearsed how they would tackle a fire, and, if they had had to enter the laboratory, a tank of powerful disinfectant would be placed in the quadrangle where they could be hosed down.

This highly specialised laboratory was eventually commissioned for use only after it had been visited and closely examined by a large number of Health and Safety Executive inspectors. Although completed and commissioned, this

Category A laboratory was never actually used. It was decided that specimens from suspected cases of highly infectious diseases in and around Edinburgh would be taken by car, followed by a relief car, to the special government laboratory at Porton Down in Wiltshire.

One of the most valuable services provided by the Bacteriology Department was a public health laboratory. For some years I worked in this laboratory. We carried out routine examinations on specimens submitted by general medical practitioners in Edinburgh and adjacent counties for infections such as scarlet fever, diphtheria, tuberculosis, glandular fever, dysentery, paratyphoid, typhoid fever, and food poisoning bacteria. One of the most dramatic episodes in the work of the laboratory was the Hawick typhoid epidemic in 1938. A number of cases occurred within a short time, which increased steadily, until over a period of several weeks, one hundred cases were diagnosed by laboratory tests. Before the discovery of penicillin and other antibiotics, typhoid fever was a very serious condition, often fatal, and indeed five people died in the Hawick outbreak. At first, specimens were brought to our laboratory, but then an emergency laboratory was set up in Hawick when the numbers continued to rise. Local public libraries were closed and public meetings were cancelled. Eventually, the continued efforts of the local public health authorities and our laboratories (at times resembling a fascinating detective story) linked all the sufferers in some way to one individual working in the catering trade.

The public health laboratory at the university also carried out similar diagnostic work for the City Fever Hospital and for what were, at one time, Edinburgh's municipal hospitals viz., the Western, Eastern, Northern and Southern General Hospitals. Unfortunately, although the technical staff carrying out this work had similar skills and professional qualifications, they were not paid salaries equal to their colleagues doing the same work in the direct employment of the National Health Service. This was a serious anomaly and a source of grievance of the staff employed by the university. Approaches were made to the university to remedy this but they were rejected. A supplement to salaries was given but this was considered inadequate. Since deadlock had been reached, I saw that the only solution was in trade union intervention. While the technical staff belonged to a professional non-negotiating body, they were not trade union members. I went to a meeting of the Transport and General Workers Union, and while it was not the most appropriate body, they were sympathetic to our cause and offered good advice. I then attended a meeting of the Edinburgh University branch of the Association of Scientific Workers, composed mainly of university academics. They were very sympathetic and persuaded their general secretary to permit the forming of a separate Edinburgh branch for medical technical staff. This took place and a significant number of my colleagues joined. A full-time organiser took up our case with the university and although not without some resistance the university agreed that appropriate university medical laboratory staff be paid on the Whitley Council scales earned by NHS employees. All this was an interesting and heartening experience.

As the chairman of our branch, I was elected as delegate to the Edinburgh Trades Council, the Edinburgh 'Parliament of Trade Unions', which met regularly in the Melbourne Halls in George IV Bridge, now long since gone. Eventually I was elected to the Executive Council of this body. It was an interesting and worthwhile experience which provided the opportunity to make many friends in the trade union world.

EIGHT

Writing and Lecturing

DURING THE Second World War there was little opportunity to become interested in Morningside's, or indeed south Edinburgh's, history. However, there is no question that my first introduction to, and stimulus to study, the subject more deeply came from a colleague in the Edinburgh world of medical laboratory technology. This was my good friend the late John Ferguson who worked, at one time, in the Royal College of Physicians' Laboratory when it was in Forrest Road and, later, in the laboratories of the Astley Ainslie Hospital and the Western General Hospital. In the first laboratory he worked with Dr Walter Levinthal, an exiled German bacteriologist, who had contributed in Berlin to the discovery of DNA.

While at the Astley Ainslie, John Ferguson asked me if I was aware of the historical background of the hospital's beautiful grounds. He drew my attention to the large ivy and tree covered mounds of earth which, at that time, were reputed (but subsequently questioned) to have been the mass burial grounds of countless, hapless Edinburgh citizens who had fallen victim to the dreaded plague or Black Death. For more than two centuries many victims of this terrible scourge, few of whom ever recovered, were brought out to this secluded part of the Burgh Muir to be quarantined in rough wooden huts built near the burial sites. John also pointed out what is traditionally believed to be the site of the small, early sixteenth-century chapel of St Roque, built by James IV, and named after the medieval European patron saint and protector of the plague-stricken.

Around 1947, when part of the hospital grounds were being excavated, I was the personal assistant of Professor T. J. Mackie, head of the University Bacteriology Department. He had asked the relevant health authorities in Edinburgh if they would permit him to take samples from the bones of the skeletons which had been uncovered, to ascertain if the plague bacilli were capable of being revived in a laboratory. Permission was not granted – much to my relief! In further discussion with John Ferguson I was fascinated to learn that in August 1513 a large part of the Scottish army had mustered here on the Burgh Muir, under the shadow of Blackford Hill and on the banks of the Jordan Burn, prior to departing for the disastrous, fatal field of Flodden. This muster is described graphically in Sir Walter Scott's dramatic work, *Marmion,* as 'between the streamlet and the town', the streamlet being the Jordan Burn which, of course, still flows past the Astley Ainslie today.

Having had my interest awakened, and having researched the above events more fully in the early 1960s, I wrote a series of articles on the subject which were published in the *Edinburgh Evening News* and other publications. Up until then there had not been a lot of recent material published on local history in Edinburgh. The exception was *Historic Morningside*, published privately by William Mair in 1947. Possibly to coincide with its publication, an exhibition on the history of Morningside was held in the parish church hall in Newbattle Terrace. This well-attended event was probably organised by Mr Mair with assistance from his fellow members of Morningside Parish Church. I clearly recall, amongst the many interesting exhibits, a damask tablecloth made by the weavers of the ancient village of Tipperlinn. This belonged to Miss Charlotte E. Evans of Morningside Park who had kindly lent it to Mr Mair for the exhibition. Miss Evans' great-grandfather was David Deuchar, the artist and engraver, who lived at Morningside House. Miss Evans' brother was an enthusiastic photographer who had taken many pictures in and around Morningside, notably the original gates to Comiston House (now at the entrance to Braidburn Valley Park) when these stood at the entrance to what is now Camus Avenue. Mr George Anderson of Morningside Park, who had been a neighbour of Miss Evans, kindly let me see, and copy, many of the photographs which her brother had taken. Unfortunately, despite Mr Anderson's invaluable help, I was unable to contact Miss Evans after she had left Morningside, presumably taking the tablecloth with her.

Quite by chance in 1977 I was approached by Mr Robin Cook (subsequently the British Foreign Secretary), who, at that time, was the assistant director of the Edinburgh Workers' Educational Association. The WEA had been running a course on the history of south Edinburgh, but sadly the lecturer had died. I was asked if I could give a course during the winter of 1977–78, consisting of sixteen lectures to cover certain areas of south Edinburgh. This appealed to me greatly, and, appreciating the invitation, I accepted. I drew up a detailed syllabus under the title 'Historic South Edinburgh' which attracted a very large enrolment at James Gillespie's High School in the autumn of 1977.

The topographical range was very wide: firstly from the Meadows, Sciennes, Grange and Whitehouse, by Bruntsfield, Greenhill, Church Hill, Tipperlinn and Morningside; then Canaan, Plewlands, Blackford, Braid and Fairmilehead; westwards to Craighouse, and Craiglockhart; and finally via Comiston, Colinton Mains, Oxgangs and Hunters Tryst to Swanston. Altogether it was quite an ambitious sweep which took many hours of preparation. At this point in my narrative, I must record, as perhaps never adequately before, that without the ready and skilled assistance of my brother, Bill, who provided a vast collection of slides, the course could not have been presented. My son, Charles, also assisted at lectures.

At such events the local historian does not usually expect to meet with embarrassment from a member of the audience, but, of course, there are always exceptions. During my first course on Historic South Edinburgh at James Gillespie's High School I was holding forth on the Burgh Muir, under the shadow of the high steeple of the Barclay Church beside the Golf Tavern. Before I could complete my description, a voice rang out, loud and clear: 'And the lecturer was born under the steeple of Barclay Church – in Glengyle Terrace'. I remained silent for a few moments to allow this historic fact to sink in and for people to take notes if necessary. I had a word with the culprit later – my father!

When I had completed the WEA course, and I was uncertain if this would be continued, I was approached by the late Basil Skinner, the highly accomplished and enthusiastic director of Edinburgh University's Department of Extra-Mural Studies (now the Department of Continuing Education), who asked me if I would consider a transfer from the WEA. I agreed to do this, as a result of which my lecturing activities then centred on the university's David Hume Tower in George Square. I was fortunate to have the assistance every week of Mr Lech Pawlowski, a class member, who transported me to and from the lecture theatre and also acted as projectionist.

A very enjoyable feature of the lecture courses were the summer walkabouts when I took the class members to visit the many places of interest seen on slides in the indoor lecture theatre. While on the part-time staff of the Extra-Mural Department, I was also pleased to assist the depart-

ment to meet its obligations to provide adult education in
Peeblesshire and other counties peripheral to the Lothians.
This involved giving a winter course of lectures on south
Edinburgh in the little schoolhouse at West Linton. Thus,
week after week, the journey was made to West Linton,
often when the weather was not ideal. Again, as on so many
other occasions, Bill acted as projectionist and also took me
out to this attractive little village as I did not have a car. We
will not readily forget the evening when, as we passed
Hillend Park and reached the fork in the road to Carlops
and West Linton, the fog became so intense that visibility
was down to a few yards. It was a frightening situation. In
an age long before mobile phones, it was impossible for us
to contact our waiting and wondering audience. But my
brother bravely, and with extreme care, drove on. Fortunately we made it and the return journey was much less
alarming.

Having undertaken considerable research, and tracked
down interesting historical material from innumerable
south Edinburgh residents, it seemed to me that it might
be worthwhile to present all the material in some kind of
publication. I thus began to assemble the contents of a
book. Writing books can be a laborious, and sometimes
even painful, process. As the age of word processors and
computers dawned, I was still writing longhand and continued to do so for many years. After my initial research in
library printed sources, I recorded facts, dates and names on
countless slips of paper, each of which was given a serial
number. After I had gathered say thirty or forty such notes
on a particular district or person, I then shuffled the slips
into chronological order, ready for writing up on ruled and
margined foolscap paper. I then gave each page a readable
sequence before having a collection of pages typed up on a
manual typewriter. The manuscript pages, initially pro-

duced from the collection of paper slips, were at first quite unreadable except by me. This meant that I had to go over them again so that the typist would be able to follow my series of PTO notes, lines and arrows pointing to other places on the page. In putting all this information together I was often dependent on the work and guidance of professional librarians, particularly so when I was doing all four volumes of *Historic South Edinburgh*. Mrs Norma Armstrong, then librarian at the Edinburgh Room of the Central Library, provided a lot of invaluable guidance and undertook the arduous task of compiling the bibliography and index. I remember that after the books were published many readers commented favourably on how well these tasks had been undertaken. A lot of effort also went into locating and copying various illustrations from existing printed material. Much of this work was done for me by Mr Malcolm Liddle in Edinburgh University's Photographic Unit in the George Square library. Outdoor photography was undertaken by my brother.

Having completed a manuscript for a possible book covering all the districts described above, I submitted this to two Edinburgh publishers. After a period of nail-biting waiting I had two rejection slips. Even in 1977 the publication of local history was not being readily undertaken by indigenous publishers. Perhaps the only exception in recent years had been *The South Side Story*, written, and published privately, by John G. Gray, with assistance from other contributors. This very successful and still popular book was first produced in 1962 with advertisements at the front and the back to defray the cost of production. Against that background, I wondered what the market would be for a local history book in 1977. It was difficult to gauge and no one seemed ready to try. Then there was one of these chance occurrences. One day in Morningside Road I met, for a matter of minutes, a good friend, the Rev. Ronald Walls, a former Church of Scotland minister who had become a convert to the Catholic Church and later a priest after his wife was tragically killed in a car crash. As Ronald hurried past he quickly enquired about my book and I told him about my rejections. Then, still hurrying, he shouted: 'Try Charles Skilton – he might be interested.' I had not heard of Charles Skilton although perhaps I should have done. He had an art studio and shop in Abbeymount and he was the owner of the Albyn Press. I made contact shortly thereafter and an appointment was made to see him on a Saturday morning. I turned up with my script in two ring binders not very professionally set out. Mr Skilton, sitting at a large desk, flicked through my manuscripts while I waited nervously. Yes, he would do it! He thought there was now a place for such local history in the Edinburgh book scene. Perhaps unwisely, I enquired if my script was too lengthy. No problem. He would publish all the available material in two volumes. So *Historic South Edinburgh* was born. I made my way from Abbeymount with the joy akin to a father having had first news of his wife giving birth.

Volume I of *Historic South Edinburgh* appeared in 1978 followed by volume II a year later. The Edinburgh reading public were kind. At a signing in Jenners I spent the whole hour autographing books for my first readers. Volume II was equally well received. While volume I was reprinted twice, volume II did not enjoy a reprint on account of the sudden death of Mr Skilton in 1989. My brother contributed a valuable chapter on the Jordan Burn in volume II, and his subsequent film, *The Jordan Burn*, made to a very professional standard, is the definitive work on Morningside's very own river.

I continued to present courses under the title 'Historic South Edinburgh' for the university's Extra-Mural Department. One of the courses I gave was entitled, 'Historic South Edinburgh: People and Places'. This seemed popular, as a result of which Charles Skilton decided to publish (as an extension to *Historic South Edinburgh*) a third and fourth volume of short biographies of famous and notable residents of south Edinburgh. Volume III, published in 1986, was devoted to people associated with the area from the Meadows to Morningside, and volume IV, published in 1988, dealt with people in the remainder of the area as far south as Swanston.

I do not think that there is any doubt that my biggest contribution to local history is contained in the four volumes of *Historic South Edinburgh*, but for various reasons I went on to complete other books which were equally interesting to do. People's interest had been aroused by the many illustrations which had come to light, either during or after my initial research. This prompted Paul Harris, author and publisher, who had taken over after the death of Charles Skilton, to publish for me a large-format book, *South Edinburgh in Pictures*, in 1989. Following that, in 1992, John Donald Publishers of Edinburgh asked me to write a summarised history and description of my own district under the title *Morningside* as a companion volume in a series of similar district histories of Edinburgh by various authors. My editor at that time was Russell Walker.

Some time after my books had been published I recall being invited to contribute to Jimmy MacGregor's morning programme on BBC Radio Scotland, when the anniversary of important events, associated with famous people who had lived in south Edinburgh, was discussed. This entailed submitting a synopsis of the subject to a BBC researcher to establish the questions which Jimmy MacGregor would ask, later, when the programme went out live. I attended the studios in Queen Street which were linked to Glasgow,

the whole interview taking place without actually meeting
Mr MacGregor in person. It all seemed rather strange to me
but I understand that it is an everyday occurrence in the
media industry where it is known as 'Down the line live'.

In addition to my lectures on south Edinburgh, I also
presented others on the general medical and public health
history of Edinburgh, including a lecture to a large audience
of the Medico-Chirurgical Society of Edinburgh in the
Symposium Hall of the Royal College of Surgeons in
Edinburgh. In 1988 my book on the history of the Astley
Ainslie Hospital was published under the title *Between the
Streamlet and the Town* (which was taken from Scott's
Marmion already referred to). That was a particularly busy
time for me as I had also been assisting Diana Sinclair to
research her book *A Sense of History*, a short account of the
Wester Hailes area of Edinburgh published in 1987. On top
of this, as a result of my appointment as archivist to the
university Medical Microbiology Department (formerly the
Bacteriology Department) I gathered material and, under
the imprint of the Wellcome Unit for the History of Medicine, had published, in 1994, *Edinburgh's Contribution to
Medical Microbiology*, edited by Emeritus Professor J. G.
Collee.

On 25 November 1995 I was the recipient of a very great
honour. This was the award of an honorary degree of
Bachelor of Science by the University of Edinburgh, my
employer for over forty years. In the citation read by the
distinguished virologist Dr John Peutherer, the then acting
head of the Department of Medical Microbiology, tribute
was paid to my service in that department, my involvement
in youth and adult community work, the books I had
written on Edinburgh, and *Edinburgh's Contribution to
Medical Microbiology* published under the imprint of the
Wellcome Unit for the History of Medicine.

The date of my graduation had to be delayed on account of the very sad and sudden death of my wife, Catherine, in July of that year. My elder daughter, Barbara (who flew over from Italy) accompanied me at the pre-Graduation dinner on the previous evening at Old College, and my younger daughter, Pauline, accompanied me at the post-Graduation lunch. My son, Charles and his wife, Maureen, kindly held a large family party in their house a few days later.

Towards the end of 1997, my very good friend, the late John Gray, advised me that he was in the process of producing a short book on a subject which had always been of great interest to him, namely, the many associations of Robert Burns with Edinburgh's south side. He had dealt briefly with the subject in his highly popular book, *The South Side Story*, more than thirty years previously, but he felt that the subject deserved more detailed treatment. John's eyesight was becoming weaker and he asked me if I would help him to complete his manuscript. I was delighted to do so. I carried out some additional research and we went on a walkabout round the district to clarify one or two outstanding queries.

After a few months, our joint publication, *A Walk on the Southside in the footsteps of Robert Burns*, appeared early in 1998, with a foreword by Burns scholar, Professor David Daiches, and many fine illustrations by Patricia Banyard. The book was launched by Mr Malcolm Cant in The Blind Poet, a hostelry in West Nicolson Street with historical associations with Robert Burns' stay in Edinburgh.

Sadly, John Gray died on 27 July 1999 shortly after his eightieth birthday. I recall that the service of thanksgiving at St Andrew's and St George's Church in George Street, conducted by the Rev. Ian Renton on 2 August 1999, was attended by a large number of people from many walks of life. During a long and active life, John Gray had been a prominent Edinburgh solicitor, a city councillor and baillie, and treasurer of the Old Edinburgh Club, among many other interests.

The time spent in what can sometimes be tedious research has its rewards, however, when I recall the many interesting personalities I have met over the years. Some years ago now, I had the interesting experience of covering the Edinburgh International Festival as a freelance reviewer and critic. This task was moderately remunerative, but the really rewarding feature was in being able, with press tickets, to enjoy many of the important and stimulating plays in the Official Festival, long before it became overshadowed, as it now seems, by the Fringe with its preponderance of stand-up comedians and their often deliberately risqué productions. For me, these early Festival years were memorable on account of being able to meet and interview many famous artistes of world renown.

Outstanding among the early theatrical events was Tyrone Guthrie's production of Robert Kemp's version of the Scottish historical masterpiece, *Ane Satyr of the Thrie Estaitis*, by Sir David Lindsay of the Mount. The highly successful production, on the apron stage of the Assembly Hall on the Mound, owed much of its attraction to Guthrie's genius. This was a landmark in the history of Scottish post-Reformation theatre. Duncan Macrae's brilliant performance still haunts the mind. Eugene O'Neill's moving masterpiece, *Long Day's Journey into Night*, in the Royal Lyceum Theatre, had a wonderful cast which included Gwen Francon-Davies, Anthony Quayle, Alan Bates and Ian Bannen. Schiller's *Mary Stuart* played to full houses, as did the thought-provoking *The Cocktail Party*, by T. S. Eliot. The Festival's international status was greatly enhanced by the French genius of mime, Jean-Louis Barrault, with the Paris Comédie Française and Juliet Greco, Jean Paul Sartre's disciple and legendary singer.

I had the privilege of interviewing a number of stars, and had dinner with Duncan Macrae who amused the waitresses with his voice and actions even off stage. I also attended a press conference at the Lyceum, during which the dynamic and chain-smoking Jean-Louis Barrault paced the floor like a tiger. When asked for his views on the future of Scottish theatre, Barrault replied that there was a rich seam of Scottish literature awaiting adaptation for the theatre or the screen, particularly James Hogg's, the Ettrick Shepherd's *Confessions of a Justified Sinner*. My friend and neighbour, Wilfred Taylor, the newspaper columnist, endorsed the French actor's suggestion in his 'Scotsman's Log', and Jack Ronder's adaptation of the play was staged at the Edinburgh Festival in the early 1970s.

Interviewing Ian Bannen after his performance in *Long Day's Journey into Night* proved to be quite an adventure. As I waited while he removed his make-up, Anthony Quayle and Alan Bates came into his dressing-room announcing, enthusiastically, that a member of the audience had called on them to suggest that O'Neill's presentation of a decaying family, apparently torn apart by each other, the father being a failed actor and the mother a recluse, was really about a family's deep love for one another. The actors felt that they had made a success. However, further discussion was curtailed when the Lyceum's caretaker suddenly appeared at the door. He was anxious to lock up and go home but Ian Bannen chose to enact for me scenes from his part in the forthcoming play, *The Iceman Cometh*, also by O'Neill. After another rattle of the keys from the caretaker, Bannen said that he would lock up and that it was in order for the caretaker to go home as it was very late.

When we finally left at 1.00 a.m., Bannen announced that he was hungry and asked where we could dine. I suggested Studio 4 in the Grassmarket, rendezvous of students and young people, which was packed to the door when we arrived. Hamish Henderson, doyen of the School of Scottish Studies, was there and had brought along some folk singers, notably his greatest discovery, Jeannie Robertson from Aberdeenshire. Unfortunately, the thick fog of tobacco smoke badly affected Jeannie, which prompted Hamish to appeal earnestly to the gathering to extinguish their cigarettes as, 'Jeannie couldna' sing for the reek'. Judging by the pall of smoke, it was going to take some time before Jeannie was able to sing. In any case it was not Ian's scene: 'Let's get out' – so we did. As a taxi drew up I remember wondering where we would go next. I decided that I would take him to our house in Jordan Lane even although I had been unable to warn my wife in advance. As we welcomed him inside, he gave the taxi driver a newspaper to read and asked him to wait, obviously with the meter still running. After demolishing a plate of sandwiches and some coffee, his form returned with a rendering of one of his favourite singers, Harry Belafonte. Ian's singing was as good as his acting. As he talked constantly of his plans for the future, I reminded him, tactfully, that the taxi fare was mounting. Yes, he'd better go. I never discovered what fare had been run up but I don't imagine he could have cared. We were privileged to have entertained a Scottish actor whose talent was matched by his courtesy and attractive personality. He had yet to become Dr Cameron in the television series, *Dr Finlay* or star in *Braveheart* (1995) and *Waking Ned* (1998) among many other films. His untimely death in a motor accident on 3 November 1999 brought widespread sadness to his many admirers.

*   *   *

Readers may have read in my other books about the origins of Morningside's biblical names, such as Jordan, Canaan, Egypt, Nile, Eden and others. Several reputable Edinburgh historians have noted the existence, in the burgh records, of the district of 'Little Egypt', the site of which was at the junction of present-day Nile Grove, Woodburn Terrace and Braid Avenue. Little (sometimes Littil) Egypt was a term frequently associated with gypsy encampments. The available evidence suggests that there was a gypsy community at Little Egypt but much of the story could be conjecture. How could one be certain when there were no definite records? I mentioned the problem to Hamish Henderson of Edinburgh University's School of Scottish Studies. Hamish, who had met many gypsies in his travels to record Scottish songs and folklore, told me that while gypsies did not usually compile written histories, they had a good wealth of family oral tradition. It was suggested that Charles Douglas, the self-styled king of the Scottish gypsies, might be able to help me. The difficulty was, of course, trying to find Charles Douglas and his gypsy community, whom I eventually located in Larkhall in Lanarkshire. Their considerable community of travelling people had links with a section of the education department of the local council. Having contacted the official concerned, I travelled by bus, one spring day, to Larkhall where I met members of the education department. One of them drove me to the camp, where Charles and his family made us most welcome in their large comfortable caravan. I told him of Morningside's Little Egypt and its history but, unfortunately, he was not really able to add much to my existing knowledge. The journey was not wasted, however, as I learned much about Scotland's travelling people. More recently, I was able to put a student in the university Scottish History department in touch with Charles Douglas and other travelling people throughout

Scotland. It has to be said that something of a mystery still surrounds the origins of Morningside's biblical names and its one-time gypsy community.

Researching local history, either to produce a book or present lectures, entails the acquisition of information and photographs, not only from books and other printed sources, but frequently from local residents. Many people, often quite elderly, have photographs, other illustrations and family archives which are unique. This type of 'leg work' can be demanding, yet rewarding, and can also, at times, have a lighter side. I once met a local resident who told me that her mother had a painting of Morningside in early times and that I could probably borrow it to make a copy. This sounded most attractive. I was just to call at the address given. I went without delay, and an elderly lady answered the door bell. I said: 'I have come about the picture.' She smiled and responded: 'Oh! I am so glad. I hoped you would come.' I was invited inside and stood waiting. Nothing happened. The lady smiled again. 'The picture,' I said. 'Do you have the picture?' 'Yes,' she said. 'Thank you.' There was still no response or sign of the picture. Finally, I asked: 'Do you have the picture?' 'Oh!' she said. 'No. I can't get it. I can get BBC1 and 2 but I can't get ITV,' slapping her television set. At last it dawned on me! I was not being greeted as a research historian but as a television repair man – someone much more important.

On Reflection

HAVING CHOSEN *Looking Back* as my title, I am bound to have found myself contrasting the past with the present. To those who lament, as many do, that: 'Things are not what they used to be,' the reply often given is: 'True, but they never were.' Reflecting upon the past and present in Morningside and beyond is bound to reveal substantial differences, but to be different is not necessarily to be better or worse.

James Grant, author of the classic work, *Old and New Edinburgh*, described Morningside in 1882 as: 'A row of thatched cottages, a line of trees and a blacksmith's forge', while other writers have added: 'and an alehouse'. Most of the trees to which Grant was referring have now gone but others have been planted. The cottages which once lined the old village street have long since been demolished and replaced by high tenements on both sides of Morningside Road. Those that remain are hidden away behind Morningside library, or at the entrance to Springvalley, or in Jordan Lane and Canaan Lane. Supermarkets have driven away many, but not all, of the original family-owned corner shops which were famed for their personal and caring approach to their customers. Building Society branch offices, cafés, restaurants (some with an oriental flavour), charity shops, gift shops, art shops and three alehouses line what must be one of the busiest and most congested arterial roads in Edinburgh. The constant stream of residents and visitors, parading up and down Morningside Road, particularly on a Saturday morning, contributes to the unique setting. For the most part, the old suburban railway line is now used only for freight trains, usually during the night, but nevertheless there is constant talk that a passenger service will be reintroduced. Nearby, 'Villadom', Robert Louis Stevenson's description of the Cluny, Midmar, Braid Road and Avenue district remains. However, the great honeycomb of servants' quarters in these large houses, which were often located either above the front door or beside the kitchen, are now used as additional living space for the residents.

In this age of fast-changing ideas on how to deal with the social problems of the day, it is also interesting to reflect on the relevance, or otherwise, of the work of the Kilbrandon Council and the experiment of the Hyve in the 1960s which I described earlier in the book. Looking back, many people would say that even if the Kilbrandon approach was right for the 1960s (which I believe it was) the world has moved on from then and the effectiveness of that approach in dealing with today's drug problems must be seriously in doubt. Nevertheless, with the decline of the uniformed youth organisations and traditional clubs, I believe that a lot of experimental work of an innovative nature is urgently required which could, perhaps, glean something from the Hyve approach.

During my long career with Edinburgh University there were many advances in medical science, and since my retirement that progress has certainly not abated. Indeed it has accelerated. The discovery of penicillin in 1928 and its production many years later, heralded a new era in the treatment of many infectious diseases. More than half a century later we are in another era where certain bacteria, some of which had been harmless have now become pathogenic and resistant to antibiotics, creating a serious cause for concern. This situation has come about partly because of the previous indiscriminate and widespread use of these anti-bacterial agents, stimulating resistance by the bacteria. Unfortunately, tuberculosis has now returned after being almost eliminated. Nevertheless, the research goes on for new therapeutic substances to control and eventually defeat a wide variety of old and new diseases.

During my own lifetime there have been enormous changes in the basic way of life of ordinary people. Many people will regret that the church bells on Sunday mornings do not now summon the substantial stream of worshippers as in previous years. Not only has this purely religious aspect of the many Morningside churches greatly diminished, but so too has the role of the churches as the focal point of the community. The churches are no longer the only centre of secular activities (if they ever were?) despite the fact that most of their organisations still remain. Nowadays, a lot of community activity and discussion centres on Morningside Association, Morningside Community Council and Morningside Heritage (Local History) Association. These bodies, rightly, attract strong support and good attendances in their quest to preserve Morningside's amenities, and to focus on local needs and problems. Many church members play an active part in these secular bodies. If the price of freedom is eternal vigilance, Morningside is fortunate that it has so many watchdogs – groups and individuals – interested in safeguarding the erosion of green space.

More widely, south Edinburgh remains a pleasant sunward area of fine houses, albeit under constant threat to its green and open spaces. The Grange Association and other similarly minded organisations are ever vigilant in protecting their area's heritage and amenities. To the west of Morningside the ancient mansion and policies of Old Craig, formerly part of the Royal Edinburgh Hospital, have been skilfully restored by Napier University. On the other side of Craiglockhart Hill, Napier University has also restored the building formerly used as the Convent of the Sacred Heart, and before that, Craiglockhart Hydropathic. Since I first wrote about it in *Historic South Edinburgh* a great deal of interest has developed in the story of the First World War poets, Siegfried Sassoon and Wilfred Owen at Craiglockhart War Hospital which was located in the same building. Today, Napier University has created a permanent War Poets' Museum and Exhibition in the former convent building.

Commendably, the district of Canaan has yielded some of its pleasant green space to provide finely-built residences for the blind. Nearby, however, the future of the beautifully situated Astley Ainslie Hospital with its ancient historic associations is not clear. It is to be sincerely hoped that whatever development takes place, the many fine and varied trees are preserved to contribute to the sense of peace that pervades this historic location.

While the physical characteristics of the area are important what really matters is the way of life of the people. Looking back, most of what created the unique features of the district still remains. This will continue to be so as long as there are people concerned and committed to ensure that Morningside and south Edinburgh remain a part of the city where children can be brought up happily in an attractive and friendly environment.

Index